COVENTRY PATMORE

COVENTRY PATMORE

by E. J. Oliver

Edward James

SHEED AND WARD • LONDON

FIRST PUBLISHED 1956
BY SHEED & WARD LTD.
33 MAIDEN LANE,
LONDON, W.C.2

PR
5143
O4

Printed in Great Britain
by Lowe & Brydone (Printers) Ltd., London, N.W.10

To the Walls

Contents

"Nunc scio quid sit amor"

—Virgil

I

Extravagant Contradictions

Independence, the quality that comes to a man who fully exercises his free will, may sometimes appear primitive and even savage in a civilised society. As its only unity is one of character, more difficult to grasp than an idea, it may seem contradictory or absurd to those unacquainted with the man in whom it is embodied.

The contradictions of which Coventry Patmore has been accused are hardly less than the contradictions in the charges themselves. A popular view of him has noticed only a minor poet, a lesser Tennyson, but even more Victorian than Tennyson; yet Gerard Manley Hopkins saw a list of popular Victorian poets which did not even mention Patmore and commented that "nothing so profound" as some poems of his could be found "in the poets of this age." Hopkins has come to be regarded as an almost twentieth-century poet, but that is one answer to the charge that Patmore was typically Victorian. On the other side it can be said that his *Angel in the House* was immensely popular and sold a quarter of a million copies in his lifetime.

Some have viewed him as a weak sentimentalist, a purveyor of sickly verses set in a Cathedral close to edify the Victorian middle class, while to others he has seemed an angry and intolerant mystic, glaring harshly at an age he hated.

These are literary aspects. His religion has been accused of similar contradictions. He has been regarded as the most

1

bigoted of Catholics, while Catholics themselves were often perturbed by his anti-clericalism. To some his religion appeared sentimental, while others were so alarmed by it that they urged him to suppress certain of his religious writings. Some found in him the unbalanced zeal of a convert, yet he made himself more at home in his Church than many born Catholics, and in fact his attitude to it was often more continental than English. He was so little of a partisan as to remark that Newman had remained Protestant in temper after his conversion and that he had always thought Keble more Catholic in outlook.

There is no more agreement about his home life. Some regarded him as the sternest of Victorian fathers, while others were charmed by his easy relations with his children, and his publisher was startled by his revolutionary idea of trying out on them all the poems he was gathering for a children's anthology. One lady was shocked by his denunciation of sentimentality to dogs, others disgusted by the privileges he accorded to his own.

Some have regarded him as typical of Victorian hypocrisy. Mr. Peter Quennell has called him "an exacting moralist, at the same time an exuberant egotist" and smiled at his "strange combination of innocence and experience." Yet he was himself a bitter critic of hypocrisy and declared that "coarseness is health" compared with some forms of suppression, adding that the young must be "hopelessly corrupt" already if they were injured by the "freest reading of the Bible or Shakespeare."

If he distressed different sorts of people, he also appealed to different sorts. Ruskin was criticized for constantly recommending his poems, while Frank Harris maintained, of a week-end spent with Patmore, that he "never enjoyed a couple of days more." Ruskin and Frank Harris were hardly similar in outlook, yet they were both admirers, while it is Harris who speaks of the "extravagant contradictions" in Patmore which so appealed to him.

Others have been less attracted by these contradictions, of which the most criticized is Patmore's passionate devotion to marriage and to three wives. It is true that his first two wives died natural deaths and the third survived him, but many have felt that three "angels in the house" damage the picture of domestic felicity shown in his famous poem.

There is yet another contradiction between his meditations on the mystery of love and his atrabilious and even cynical judgment on human nature: "Ninety-nine men in a hundred are natural men, that is, beasts of prey." He also published passages of the most intimate tenderness, yet was alive to the indiscretion of putting these before a large public, for, he said, "Popular esotericism—and esotericism is becoming popular—means conscientious wenching or worse."

Conscientious wenching? There is certainly a type of mysticism prevalent since his day which is open to this charge. Unfortunately this is also the charge most commonly brought against Patmore himself. Even those most in sympathy with his general ideas have called him a "flirt" and wondered at his devotion to ideal womanhood which still enabled him to bury two wives, marry a third, nor remain quite indifferent to the gifts or charms of other women.

This too has been seen as a form of Victorian hypocrisy, yet his admirers value him largely for his criticism of hypocrisy and of the puritan society around him. In one or two fundamentals he went deeper than Carlyle, Ruskin, or even Matthew Arnold in criticism of his age, though he lacked their range.

This list of contradictions, though not exhaustive, is bewildering enough, but the variety of them at least indicates the independence of Patmore's character. He can hardly be called typical of his age, his Church, or his country, when he was so open to criticism by all of them. He stands out from the crowd by a certain erectness of carriage and idiosyncrasy of mind, as a Johnson stands out from the urbane salons of the eighteenth century or a Danton from the tumbrils of the Revolution. If it was not given him to dominate and control events or movements of the mind, he preserved his independence, resisting the prejudices of his age and country, or transforming them in such a way that they became more characteristic of him than of his background.

His independence was the more striking because it was his fate to be isolated in a moral climate unsympathetic to his passionate nature and in an age increasingly doubtful of his absolute convictions. He was a firm believer in simplicities which were out of fashion, regarding it as his chief work to uncover the primitive revelation originally made to all mankind, which he believed was to some extent repeated in every generation, "a state of fire-mist, which a due meditation on the Incarnation would condense into New Heavens and a New Earth."

Many of the apparent contradictions in him arise simply from his independence. Edmund Gosse said of his appearance that he was "exceedingly unlike other men." The remark, true enough of the tall figure with humour in the eyes and wilful sensuality in nose and mouth, can be applied to the whole man, and he was most unlike other men in the distinctions he made: as a poet he was profound in thought, but simple in expression, his aim being "gaiety of manner with gravity of matter"; he disciplined his children, yet indulged their ambitions; he mourned those he loved, yet never buried his own heart; he suffered, yet declared that "life is not only joyful, it is joy itself."

These are distinctions which can also be viewed as contradictions, yet in reality Patmore's character was neither complex nor contradictory; it was in fact his intransigence, the very straightness of his growth, which made him appear so difficult. He gave no concessions and, not imposing on himself any philosophical system which did not correspond to the deepest desires of his heart, he presented to the world the twisted ramifications of an oak-tree, complex in appearance, but an entirely natural growth: *The Rod, the Root, and the Flower*, the title of his most brilliant work, has the same unity and the same apparent disorder.

If he cannot be regarded as a model Victorian, nor a representative Englishman, nor a Catholic saint, his status as a lover may also be open to question. Yet here at least he was wholly typical, for he was a wonderful example of human nature. This is his real attraction, that while he had gifts which made him outstanding, his human qualities and problems were those which appear in the majority of men, but what they commonly hide, he revealed. Many would agree with him that the vision of childhood and the awakening of love before the age of twenty was "all the light of all their day," but few make this the basis of their life and judge everything in that light. Many try to follow their heart and to obey their conscience, but few reach the point at which the two meet. As a lover Patmore had the courage to admit that he had been in paradise, the courage "not to deny in the darkness, what he had seen in the light." He had the simplicity and the gratitude to confess his happiness. To a common human experience he gave an intensity which is more often felt than expressed, and asserted that it was in the depths of his emotions that man realised the touch of the divine.

He had what is sometimes called a happy nature, but which is often no more than a simple one, having an interior gaiety independent of circumstances. He was simple in his personal optimism, which was a constant source of amusement to his friends. His children were always the most remarkable of children, his house the most convenient; the dinners he attended always produced the most brilliant talk to which he listened with amazement; the very flowers and animals around him were always prize specimens. He lived in a world of superlatives. The superlatives appeared as often when he talked of popular ideas, the trend of the times and especially politics; but here he always indulgèd an extreme pessimism. He lived in the best of houses, but in the most deplorable of ages. His friends constantly noted the contrast between his personal optimism and his pessimism with regard to the world.

This is perhaps the trait of an egotist, but not an unamiable one. The egotistical are too often confused with the selfish. Patmore was generous and kindly, but he stood very much at the centre of his world; and this too can be the mark of a simple nature. Such optimism and such pessimism are normal enough, but in Patmore they were intensified; he had indeed that intensified appetite for the normal which some have held to be a privilege of genius.

In one particular his destiny was different from that of most men, but this particular was so important that it has greatly added to the difficulty of understanding him. Once more it concerns his three marriages, but it was not only that he married three times. It is more true to say that he had three lives.

The most peculiar fact is that he lived almost the same number of years with each of his three wives, nearly fifteen years with his first wife, over fifteen years with his second, and he had already lived just over fifteen years with his third when he died in 1896.

This is an odd enough occurrence in one man's life, but what is stranger still is that his work falls naturally into the same three periods of time, fifteen years each. In the reign of his first wife, he wrote *The Angel in the House;*

the great poem, simple and even banal, though with its depths, which was so popular with the Victorian public. In the time of his second wife he wrote *The Unknown Eros,* the mystical poems which were first disregarded and then admired by the intellectuals who had been inclined to smile at *The Angel.* Under the dispensation of his third wife he wrote the essays and aphorisms which are certainly the most perfect expression of his thought and perhaps his most valuable contribution to literature.

He could not have shown his devotion to his wives more exactly than by dividing his life and work into three different departments, each under the sign of a distinct muse. Yet he could hardly have planned his life with such accuracy; only the subtlest of murderers could have contrived the death of two wives, and even his sharpest critics have not accused him of murder. The answer to the problem should perhaps be sought in the character of the wives themselves.

Yet these were not all remarkable women. The first, Emily Patmore, who exercised the most influence on him, was very much a devoted Victorian wife and mother. She had a clear and intelligent beauty, admired by Tennyson, Ruskin and the Pre-Raphaelites who came to the house. She was unusual in that she had both qualities which endeared her to the man who loved her, and their children, and those which allow a woman to sit among artists without being either too strident or too withdrawn, more ready to appreciate than to shine herself. She had the gifts of a listener, and she listened to one of the longest poems of the age, *The Angel in the House,* which had something of her own discretion.

The second Mrs. Patmore was described by Patmore himself as "the pure effulgence of Catholic Sanctity." She was very reserved and shy, and had taken a vow never to marry, from which she was dispensed. It was under her gentler sway that Patmore wrote *The Unknown Eros.*

The third Mrs. Patmore was more worldly. She was previously governess to his children, and so gained access to his heart. She had wit and she exercised great care over his reputation and over his papers. It was perhaps right that while married to her he should have written his prose, but this was among his most exalted and most mystical work.

So similar contradictions appear when the characters of his wives are set beside the character of his work. Their inspiration is obvious, but they inspired creations which were in some respects the opposite of themselves. His first wife gave her discretion to *The Angel in the House,* but this achieved a vulgar popularity which was the opposite of her modesty. The second wife gave her sanctity to *The Unknown Eros,* but its outspokenness was the opposite of her timidity and reserve. The third wife inspired him to write prose, but this had a fervour which was the opposite of her worldliness.

In the end, therefore, despite the three orderly phases of fifteen years and the work produced under three different inspirations, Patmore reveals the same trait in relation to his wives as in relation to his Church, his country or his period. Even when he was most dependent on them for his inspiration, it was his nature to react, to assert his independence. Indeed, his whole philosophy of love was founded on the tension between masculine and feminine. He who praised woman as the angel in the house and aimed to serve a higher conception of ideal womanhood than any poet since Dante was also, of all men, the man who spoke most strongly against the domination of men by women. An anti-clerical Catholic, he was also an anti-feminist lover.

Yet, once more, these contradictions had nothing affected in them; so far from seeking to be extravagant he was fundamentally as simple in his character as in his tastes—once he said that he believed he could spend an income of £75,000 a year and still maintain austerity and simplicity in his household. In the same style he was able to maintain the simplicity of his character through all the extravagant contradictions which others have seen in him. If the independence of his character forced him to react against the ideas of his age as naturally as against the feminine temperaments of the women in his life, it was only because he remained so true to his heart.

Others have reacted against the Victorian age, a whole generation in fact, which is now attempting to strike a balance between what it wishes to reject and what it wishes to retain. Coventry Patmore once said that he had respected posterity and dared to hope that it would respect him; it has so far respected him that it has repeated his own experience, and we are now, perhaps for the first time, in a position to observe his life without prejudice.

II

Father of the Man

Coventry Patmore was born at Woodford in Essex on July 23rd, 1823. It is believed that he acquired the name of Coventry from a godmother, the Hon. Mrs. Coventry. It proved an appropriate one, for there was a stage in his life when it might well have been a nickname, as his isolation was such that he had the appearance of being "sent to Coventry" in the republic of letters, a tribute to that independence of character which was always his outstanding quality.

The custom of naming a child after a godparent was one that he retained for his own children, calling the eldest Milnes after Richard Monckton Milnes, and the next Tennyson after the poet. It is a custom which avoids the vagaries of fashion, but not those of friendship, and the second child long survived the intimacy between Patmore and Tennyson.

The unknown godmother, the Hon. Mrs. Coventry, also provides an introduction to Coventry's father, Peter George Patmore, a man to value such connections with the lesser titles of the aristocracy while respecting and cultivating higher values in the literature of his age. He was the sort of person, common then and not wholly vanished today, who, genuinely devoted to the arts, finds them even more attractive when they open the doors of fashion and confer a certain status in society. A dandy, received by Lady Blessington, he was preserved from the more ordinary forms of snobbery by the fact that he was also something of a Bohemian, independent in his literary judgments and in his friendships, even to the point of indiscretion.

His indiscretions have indeed somewhat obscured his reputation, of the sort that is considerable in life but quickly extinguished by death. His indiscretions alone were considerable enough to outlive him. If anybody thought it worth while to compose a biography of him, he would probably describe him as "the friend of Hazlitt." He was a good friend, and the first of the indiscretions held against him is that it was to him that Hazlitt wrote some of the tormented letters caused by his unhappy love affair, later published as *Liber Amoris*. In this Hazlitt wrote at some length of his passion for his landlady's daughter, a girl who teased him with her charms without giving him any intimate enjoyment of them. It was unusual at that time for a married man, as Hazlitt was, to publish an account of his love affair with another woman, without even the mask of fiction; and as this account took the form of letters written to two friends, of whom one was Peter George Patmore, he was censured hardly less severely than Hazlitt himself. He had lacked strength to protest at the indiscretion of publishing such a book, but he had the strength to champion Hazlitt and to assert that he was chiefly vilified because he was "the most original thinker of his day" and the only intellectual who remained faithful to the ideas of the French Revolution.

But Hazlitt's *Liber Amoris* long failed to achieve the indulgence it deserved. There was a real pathos in the conquest of a man of genius by a chit of a girl, but it was a pathos for which nineteenth-century England lacked sympathy. The elder Patmore was blamed for his connection with it, and when the book itself appeared in 1823—the affair it described had taken place in 1820—he was particularly vulnerable to criticism, for his reputation had not recovered from an unfortunate part he had played in a duel.

In 1821 Peter George Patmore, who suffered so much in seconding the literary efforts of his friends, was actually second in a duel in which his principal was killed. This arose from a complex quarrel between the *London Magazine* and *Blackwood's*. John Scott and John Gibson Lockhart, the son-in-law and biographer of Sir Walter Scott, were the parties originally involved—there was of course no relationship between the two Scotts, and the quarrel was quite confused enough without this similarity of name. John Scott was editor of the *London Magazine,* and the quarrel ultimately turned on the extent to which Lockhart was the responsible editor of *Blackwood's*. In Lockhart's absence he was represented by his friend Christie, who had Traill to act as his second, while John Scott's second was Peter George Patmore.

Duelling was already becoming obsolete in England, and these literary gentlemen were determined to be chivalrous, but their seconds had more loyalty to their principals than knowledge of duelling. This comic mixture of chivalry and ignorance resulted in tragedy. The duellists met on a February evening—Christie said afterwards that he had only chosen the evening because he wanted to get the affair over as quickly as possible. There was some uncertainty about the light and the position of vantage. Both principals wished to be scrupulously, even chivalrously fair, and Christie, acting only for Lockhart and having no direct interest in the quarrel, fired his first shot in the air. It was then that the two seconds, worried both by the danger to their friends and the uncertainty of the light, began to lose their heads. When the pistols had been reloaded, Christie's second, Traill, called out, "Now, Mr. Christie, take your aim, and do not throw away your advantage as you did last time." Scott then said to Patmore, "What, did not Mr. Christie fire at me?" Patmore replied, "You must not speak: you have nothing for it but firing."

A second shot was fired. Scott was wounded and died ten days later.

Both seconds were evidently flustered and incompetent, but it was Christie's second, Traill, who was more at fault. He should have formally announced to Patmore that his principal had fired in the air and enquired whether Scott was satisfied, as of course he would have been. But Patmore might well have intervened, if he had really heard Traill's remark—although he afterwards maintained that he had not caught the words and thought that the others were complaining of the light. As it was, a death was caused by ignorance of etiquette on one side and by etiquette on the other.

In the event Patmore was more blamed, simply because his principal died, but Scott's widow never blamed him and held Traill responsible.

The account given above was the one accepted at the inquest, but of course neither the unfortunate Scott nor Patmore, who had left the country and was hiding in Calais under the names of "P. G. Pitt" and "P. G. Preston," was there to say what he had heard or not heard.

This duel left a mark on the elder Patmore's reputation from which it never quite recovered. Once more he had to suffer for loyalty to his friends. He also suffered for loyalty to his literary opinions, for he was sharply criticized for praising Keats and Shelley when they were still objects of ignorance or contempt. It was an amiable if less admirable trait in his loyalty that he more often followed his friends into trouble than kept them out of it.

Yet some good came of the duel, which indirectly led to

the birth of Coventry Patmore, for it is doubtful whether Peter George would have married at all, if it had not been for the disturbance caused by the duel in his peaceful bachelor existence. It was not until his return from Calais that he finally fell in with his mother's wishes and married a young Scotswoman, Eliza Robertson, whom she had introduced into the house for that purpose.

It was his mother's doing: she used this crisis in his affairs to bring about the match. A woman of great character and affection, she was anxious to become a grandmother, and it was she who provided Coventry with far more warmth and affection than the woman she had chosen to be his mother. Yet it may not have been an unwise choice, for the young Scotswoman had exactly the sterner qualities which her husband lacked. Indeed, it was only the shock of the duel which induced him to settle down with such a woman. It was that sort of a marriage, very different from the nuptial bliss which their son was to celebrate.

Coventry seems to have had much more in common with his father's than with his mother's family, whose puritanism certainly attended his first steps in religion, but only to send him in reaction to the reading of Catholic theology. His grandfather, the husband of his remarkable Patmore grandmother, had been a jeweller; late in life Coventry Patmore developed a passion for jewels and acquired some of a connoisseur's knowledge, nor is it altogether fanciful to see a hereditary trait in the careful craftsmanship of his verse. But the grandmother who had arranged his parents' marriage and so prepared his coming into the world was a much stronger influence—and one that persisted, for she lived to the age of ninety-three. Yet she had not only vitality but a tenderness which does not always go with it. She once wrote to her grandson that she thought of him "every day" and "every hour." In contrast to Coventry's own mother, she had those maternal feelings which mothers have not always the leisure or the simplicity, even if they have the temperament, to express openly to their children.

Peter George Patmore's third indiscretion, after his connection with Hazlitt's book and the duel, was to speculate disastrously in railways shares during the boom of the 'forties, then once again leave the country, with the result that Coventry and his brother, after a carefree youth, were left penniless except for a sum enclosed in the letter announcing the disaster.

The fourth and last indiscretion of the elder Patmore was to publish, in 1854, *My Friends and Acquaintances,* a book of memoirs which provoked the critics; and this appeared just before the first part of his son's great work, *The Angel in the House.* The affair of the duel was revived and this last indiscretion sealed the reputation of the elder Patmore, who died in the following year.

His indiscretions have been put first, not only for their public effect and importance in the lives of father and son, but because they illustrate one side of a character which was in many respects lovable. The worst that can be said of the father only shows up his many good qualities, as it is evident that the worst he suffered was in the cause of friendship, for which he had a very real talent. His son resembled him in this, though less sociable by nature and having more friends than acquaintances. People often smiled at the vigour with which Coventry Patmore championed his friends, even to the extravagance of asserting that first Herrick, and then Goethe, were nothing but "brilliant insects" when compared with a versifier he particularly cherished. Unfortunately Victorian discretion has concealed the identity of the friend so extravagantly praised.

The elder Patmore had one supreme merit in friendship which only a writer can appreciate at its true value, for he used his influence with editors to see that his friends were paid promptly, and even arranged an advance for Hazlitt on a course of lectures. Such virtue alone should admit him to the Elysian fields of literature.

But this virtue was most strikingly revealed in his behaviour to his son Coventry, for he positively rejoiced to discover that he was a poet, and gave him every encouragement, and this in a bourgeois household around which were rapidly rising the prosaic standards of Victorian England. He loved poetry and he loved his son—perhaps only this double love made possible such virtue in a father.

His indiscretions could indeed be defended as a form of unworldliness, remarkable in a man who had been a dandy and a frequenter of fashionable salons. He was very much a man of the Regency, which looked back to the eighteenth century and had little in common with the· Victorian era; his years of success as a writer, from 1825 to 1845, were after the Regency, but in spirit he belonged to the earlier years, for, as occurs with most men of letters, his world remained the one he had known when he was still a young man of twenty. He preserved another trait of the eighteenth century, its scepticism, and gave his children no religious teaching. Yet even towards the other world he displayed the same amiable and civilised qualities which he had in this one, and showed respect to the Bible; his respect for literature was perhaps the basis of his character.

The Patmore household contained the classics of literature which Coventry read and discussed with his father, who formed a high opinion of his gifts and even insisted on the publication of his first poems at the age of twenty-one. One of the few poems among these which he later republished was

"The Woodman's Daughter," written at the age of sixteen; it concludes with a reference to

> . . . drifting mists, thro' which the moon is
> riding like a ghost,

and only the ghost of his later poetry is to be discerned in it. For in spite of his precocity his mastery continued to develop up to the publication of *The Unknown Eros* in 1877, when he was fifty-four; and some would even maintain that his most characteristic work was in the prose written between that date and his death in 1896 at the age of seventy-three.

Yet these first poems were praised by responsible critics, not only friends of the father such as Leigh Hunt. Browning and Thackeray were among those favourably impressed. There was also hostility, especially from *Blackwood's*, which saw in the verses "the slime" of Shelley and "Keates" whose name—in 1844—was still spelt wrongly.

It is probable that without the elder Patmore's influence these verses would never have been published, a fact which underlines his indulgence for his son. Certainly Coventry Patmore always cherished the memory of his father and was indignant over any reference to his indiscretions. This was not only filial but just, for he had his share of the father's indiscretion, but he also had a much stronger character, so that in him indiscretion was elevated to independence and an aloofness from the world; yet that characteristic independence had its roots in the father's attitude to life which, however weak, was never mean, nor shaken by the world's literary standards.

Coventry Patmore also had from his father eighteenth-century standards of aristocratic culture, which became more marked in later life. Altogether his debt to his father was considerable and one which he was always the first to emphasize.

The father was not only responsible for his love and respect for literature in youth, but also for the reverence, which developed just as early, that he always held for the vocation of poet: the tendency to spell the words with a capital letter—the Poet, the Seer. It is in this character that he stands in the portrait which Sargent painted at the end of his life, showing a quality which also led Sargent to do a sketch of him as the prophet Ezekiel for a large group in the Boston Library. The elder Patmore, the dandy, and the son, the prophet, had a quality in common: they both regarded the world with a certain aloofness.

One practical step which the father took in the education of his son, sending him to Paris with the object of improving his French, also had an important effect on his development as a poet, for he fell in love with an English girl, the daughter of a well-known novelist, Mrs. Gore, who had a salon in the Place Vendôme. The girl was eighteen; he was sixteen. He was passionately adoring, she supercilious.

To be in love in Paris at the age of sixteen is an experience that might well make a lover find an enchantment in the city itself and introduce the Seine into the main stream of his life. On Patmore it had the opposite effect, perhaps due to the mockery of the girl, for he was the last man to enjoy the part of a hopeless lover. For him reciprocity was the essence of love, and he detested melancholy.

But a young lover finds it hard to resist melancholy, and there is little doubt that Paris was for him a place of tears and sighs. Too devoted a lover to blame the girl, he resented Paris and the French instead, a feeling reinforced by the traditional English enmity to France. Such prejudices were not infrequent in him but usually, as in this case, they went deeper than the personal mood which provoked them, for he had an intuition in such matters. He really disliked the French, and especially the Parisians, for the frivolity of their loves and their cynical maxims about women. Later he was particularly indignant over the remark that there were not more than about twenty-five species of women. If the senses of the man who made it had not been "Frenchified," he scornfully commented, he would have realised that "every woman is a species in herself—nay, many species." Doubtless he was unjust to the French, for it was an English girl who had mocked him with the heartlessness of Paris, but there had probably been French onlookers to observe his discomfort with intelligent malice.

When he returned to Paris on the way to Rome, after the death of his first wife, he found little to admire in the Louvre and asserted that the British Museum had a finer Venus than the Venus of Milo. Later still, when he was a Catholic, it is true that he admitted, "from a Christian point of view, we English are a very poor lot compared with the French," but even this did not alter his general attitude. He only went to Lourdes very much against his will, in a deliberate effort of self-sacrifice. In this he was richly rewarded, but his devotion to the Mother of God did not extend to Notre Dame de Paris.

Yet it was in the city under her protection that an English girl first set him on the way which led both to *The Unknown Eros* and to Lourdes, for it was at this time that he wrote his first poems and even conceived the first idea of devoting his gifts to the praise of marriage. However much he misjudged Paris, he always remained grateful to Miss Gore, and when he later discovered a portrait that resembled her he set it on the wall behind shutters and, to those intrigued by the mystery, admitted that behind those shutters was "the first Angel."

It is a Frenchman, Giraudoux, who has said that the woman we love is always the same woman. It is exactly the sort of remark that Patmore would have resented, but it has a bearing on him. He was an enthusiastic reader of Plato as a young man, and there are passages in his later prose which have a clear Platonic echo, nor is it unusual in a young man to have a Platonic idea of woman which he attaches to the one nearest, not always the most worthy of it. It is, according to one's indulgence, the pathos or the absurdity of Patmore that he retained this faculty for falling in love all his life, while never really being capable of Platonic love.

This aspect of his character will emerge more fully when we consider his marriages, but nobody will have much sympathy for him who fails to realise that his whole life was divided between strong physical passion and a passion for fidelity, in accordance with a vision of the other world. Such stresses, and the attempt to resolve them, commonly bring today the charge of hypocrisy, levelled against other eminent Victorians. Some hypocrisy there always is in a man who tries to control his passions and sets his mind on an object outside himself. His critics can always say that these efforts are not the real man; but hypocrisy of this sort is the stuff of human nature. What was unusual about Patmore was that the forces on both sides were exceptionally violent and that he consistently sought to sublimate rather than to suppress his desires.

As a young man between the years of sixteen and twenty he found in himself both the passions of this world and visions of the other, for his time in Paris was followed by a period of religious questioning which culminated in a visit to Edinburgh, at the age of nineteen, to his mother's family, members of the Free Kirk. He was impressed by their piety but painfully embarrassed at being expected to give testimony of the faith that was in him, an ordeal which left him tongue-tied. He was also acquainted with fear and horror of Rome and Catholicism; and he records in the fragment of autobiography which he wrote in later life at the suggestion of Gerard Manley Hopkins that he prayed earnestly against this insidious foreign religion.

But ever after that visit to Edinburgh he remained deeply interested in religion; already he saw human love in terms of the divine, and it is probable that his awakening to the one in Paris also quickened interest in the other, so that Paris and Edinburgh, those old allies, between them had a decisive influence on the man who always had something of a prejudice against France and Scotland.

He was not unusual in having love and religion enter his life together, but while with most men one or the other usually takes control, so that they are dominated either by their emotions or by their sense of duty, in him they became fused to such an extent that while some were edified or amused by the extravagance of his devotion to a woman, others were startled or shocked by the passionate nature of his religion.

Certainly a decisive element in his life entered it at the age of nineteen, though it is not easy to fix exactly what it was, for he referred to it many years later in writing of his first visit to Lourdes in 1877, when he said that "the prayers of thirty-five years" had been answered. That goes back to 1842, when he was nineteen. But he always said that he went to Lourdes because he had been lacking in devotion to the Mother of God. He could hardly have prayed for an increase in this particular devotion when he was under the influence of the Free Kirk and filled with a horror of Rome. It is evident that the devotion also symbolized for him the solution of some inner conflict which had troubled him since the age of nineteen. It is easy enough to speculate on the virtue which a passionate young man would find hardest to acquire, but the reference suggests some doubt or difficulty of a more intellectual nature. Clearly it concerned the relations between love and religion which preoccupied him then and for his whole life. A fuller examination of this problem (see Chapter VIII) suggests that it may have turned on the question of virginity, for in the fervour of his desire to glorify marriage—and already he was considering himself as the poet of marriage—he may have refused to see any virtue in virginity.

Whatever the exact nature of the crisis, it is clear that at the age of nineteen his thought fixed itself on the chief interest of his life. He once quoted with approval "one of the few really good things ever said by Hazlitt"—the note of asperity towards Hazlitt being doubtless due to the harm done to the elder Patmore's reputation by the *Liber Amoris*. Hazlitt's remark was that "men of genius spend their lives in teaching the world what they themselves learned before they were twenty." The implication is that it was true of Coventry Patmore himself, though it also fits his whole conception of genius, which he regarded as a sort of primitive revelation, declaring that most children are geniuses before they acquire moral and intellectual responsibilities, which so often disorder the conscience and cloud the vision.

Such responsibilities, increased at the age of twenty-two by the sudden change in his existence brought about by his father's speculation in railway shares, narrowed his own genius. In those last years of freedom in his father's household, his mind had revolved in many different spheres of interest; first he had read the poets and Plato, then turned to painting and won an award from the Royal Society of Arts for a copy of a painting by Landseer; in Paris he had learnt more German than French in talk at the school he attended, and had also become a fair fencer; then at home he had studied theology, considered taking orders, but instead had a laboratory fitted up in which he conducted chemical experiments with some competence, though Gosse remarked that he would have preferred Faraday's opinion on some of the claims that Patmore made for them; finally at the age of twenty-one he had his first poems published. It is a brilliant range of interests, almost equalling the Renaissance Florentines in its variety and fully illustrating his own belief that there is a genius in youth which passes with the coming of maturity.

There was all this behind him when he came of age, a young man who had been something of a prodigy, indulged by a father who had given him a fine taste in literature and introduced him to a circle of friends where, according to his father, he remained outside the brilliant talk, perhaps with that quizzical expression which is so evident in the Brett drawing of him made some years later. This shows an extremely handsome young man with delicately moulded features, some sensuality in the nostrils and mouth, but the whole drawing is dominated by the humourous detachment in the eyes, without any trace of the Byronic arrogance revealed in the Sargent portrait of him painted at the end of his life. Yet in both drawing and portrait, some forty years apart, the quizzical expression is the same: clearly there was a humour to counterbalance both the sensuality of youth and the arrogance of age. Photographs taken earlier than the portrait also confirm this attractive quality, showing that the arrogance was only intellectual, the defiance of strong convictions. All likenesses reveal the same independence of attitude.

When he was twenty-two, his father's money troubles and flight to France also forced him to seek an independence in material things; for over a year he earned not much more than a pound a week by translating and writing for the reviews. Once when he was down to his last shilling he

B

spent this on ices, to find payment for an article awaiting him on his return to his room.

In this difficult situation, the virtues of the father, whom some might blame for bringing up a son to leisure and abandoning him at the moment when he needed a start in life, once more outweighed his faults, for his friends helped the son and it was at the home of one of them that Coventry Patmore encountered Monckton Milnes, the patron of Victorian letters, a man with the elder Patmore's readiness to help writers and the same passion for literature, but considerably more endowed with character and means to help. He was the more eager to assist because he had enquired of the hostess who the young man with the frayed cuffs was, but he soon read his poems, and made amends for the slighting remark by getting Patmore a job at the British Museum. All this was a consequence of the elder Patmore's gift for friendship, and there is a poetic justice in the father's services to literature being rewarded in the son; a more worldly father, who committed no indiscretions, would probably have made a poet's life much more difficult.

Two years after he had taken up his post at the British Museum, Coventry Patmore became engaged to Emily Augusta Andrews, daughter of a Congregational minister. He was twenty-three, she a year younger. He proposed on Hampstead Heath and they were married in the same year at Hampstead church. This was the felicity of his life and also its tragedy, for when she died he was constantly trying to replace her.

III

Before The Angel

Emily Augusta Patmore, "by whom and for whom I became a poet," as Patmore later wrote, had been modelled by fate not only to be the "Angel in the House" of his poem, but also to be the muse of a literary and artistic circle. She had sweetness, beauty, and poise.

The portrait which Millais painted of her in 1851, four years after the marriage, reveals a beauty which is impressive, having dignity without excessive pride. There is a great seriousness in the large eyes, intelligence in the shape of the face, yet the effect is more of sweetness than austerity.

Browning wrote a poem to her which, under the title of "A Face," is one of the better known of his shorter poems:

If one could have that little head of hers
　　Painted upon a background of pale gold,
Such as the Tuscan's early art prefers!
　　No shade encroaching on the matchless mould
Of those two lips, which should be opening soft
　　In the pure profile; not as when she laughs,
For that spoils all: but rather as if aloft
　　Yon hyacinth, she loves so, leaned its staff's
Burthen of honey-coloured buds to kiss
And capture 'twixt the lips apart for this.
Then her lithe neck. three fingers might surround,
How it should waver on the pale gold ground

Up to the fruit-shaped, perfect chin it lifts!
I know, Correggio loves to mass, in rifts
Of heaven, his angel faces, orb on orb
Breaking its outline, burning shades absorb:
But these are only massed there, I should think,
Waiting to see some wonder momently
Grow out, stand full, fade slow against the sky
(That's the pale ground you'd see this sweet face by),
All heaven, meanwhile, condensed into one eye
Which fears to lose the wonder, should it wink.

Coventry and Emily Patmore had settled down in High-gate, where Browning was only one of the visitors to her court, though these verses of his were the most memorable entry in the album of this period. Tennyson was a more frequent visitor and Patmore's closest friend in these early years of his married life. Friends of the elder Patmore and those of Monckton Milnes led naturally to these and other friendships, while young writers and artists, most of them still bachelors, appreciated a household where intelligence and beauty were happily married.

Yet it was neither Browning nor Tennyson who was really most representative of that Highgate life, which owed more to an intellectual tradition associated with two writers of prose, one an English art critic who had already become the arbiter of taste, the other an American thinker and essayist who was to dominate English intellectual circles in which ethics were a passion stronger than religion. Ruskin and Emerson were the giants of those days. Coventry and Emily Patmore had both admired Emerson before their marriage, and the revelation of this to each other had been one of the seals set on their love.

Ruskin and Emerson not only represented new ideas: they were the type of a new civilisation. Those who had acquired prosperity and leisure from the Industrial Revolution were in need of new masters and new houses, distinct from the bland voices of the Establishment and the aristocratic terraces of the eighteenth century. Moving out of London—from a city where they had made enough money and from the more fashionable western districts whose frivolity they despised—such people built houses in agreeable villages which in the course of the century became the prosperous suburbs of outer London. These houses were solid. Outwardly they were protected by thick shrubberies, plush and lace curtains. Inwardly they reposed no less firmly on the foundations of Ruskin and Emerson, who supplied the new heaven for their new earth. Browning had come from Camberwell, one of these villages to the south of London, and Ruskin himself from the neighbouring village of Dulwich. Highgate and Hampstead on the northern heights of London, housed others who observed the same respectable tradition. These people, with a bourgeois culture of their own, were devout in their admiration for Ruskin and Emerson. They were austere and held aloof from fashion. They believed fervently in the ethical value of literature, and they admired art in so far as they could find the same value in it. Art excited them, yet they were distrustful of its southern nudities and colours, even a little distrustful of those who were so raffish as to live a mile or two south of themselves.

That was the world in which the Patmores lived, but they were not entirely of it. They had even gone as far as the south coast for their honeymoon, to Hastings, a town to which Patmore remained devoted all his life and in which he was one day to build a Catholic church. They returned to settle in Highgate, but they were not rich enough to strike the flourishing roots proper to such neighbourhoods. They had moves forced on them by the arrival of children, the necessities of economy and health. Even when they owned a house, they had to let it and live in furnished rooms to save money. They went down to Hampstead and even as far down as Bloomsbury, which was convenient for the British Museum where Patmore worked. Yet through all these changes they remained faithful to their world, which had its newly established masters but also its independence.

In that world the social conventions were firm, but these people who had avoided revolutions were nevertheless able to be independent, which sometimes required more strength. Patmore was one day to escape almost entirely from that atmosphere, but at least it was one which encouraged such freedoms; it too, hardly less than his father, had its contribution to make towards his independence.

From Highgate Patmore went daily to his work at the Museum library, and returned in the evening to supplement his income by writing for the reviews. His wife watched over his ambition and had her own anxiety for his career, by which she understood not these daily tasks but his vocation as a poet. That, it had been agreed between them, was his true destiny; it was even that which had led Monckton Milnes to secure him his bread-and-butter job at the Museum. Poetry then naturally dominated the lives of the young couple, and time had to be made for this third and most important of his tasks, after the day's work and the evening's column had been done. Fortunate in his father, Patmore was no less fortunate in his wife, who was so devoted to his vocation that she even put up with surrender of their home life to assist his real work.

Almost as important was the use she made of the home as a centre for his friends, who were evidently attracted by her qualities hardly less than by his own. He had a gift for friendship that never lacked friends, but after her death these were not always the same ones. His conversion, and changes in himself and others, partly explain this, but the fact at least shows that such men as Browning and Tennyson went to see the Patmores, not only their fellow-poet. Against this, Carlyle and Ruskin remained friends of Patmore's throughout their lives.

It was to be expected that such men as Carlyle and Ruskin, whose thought and personality so impressed themselves on their age and country, would have considerable influence on Patmore in their visits to his house at this time. But though he respected them, and friendly feelings and correspondence survived all the changes in his life, there is little evidence that their outlook affected his. Of all his elders, Patmore certainly had most respect for Carlyle, but though he shared some of Carlyle's opinions, the sympathy between them was also a matter of temperament and a common religious attitude towards life.

Apart from Carlyle, Patmore matured in a world chiefly influenced by Ruskin and Emerson; but while Ruskin was a most enthusiastic admirer of *The Angel in the House* and Emerson was its no less zealous champion in America, where it achieved success earlier than in England, Patmore even before his wife's death had been less influenced by their teaching than by the reading of traditional theology. He welcomed Ruskin's attacks on the materialists and the philistines, just as he had much sympathy with Carlyle's emphasis on personal authority, but such principles were far too integral to him to require support from outside.

It is clear from his correspondence with them that neither Ruskin nor even Carlyle dominated him in life as they have risen above him in subsequent literary history. Ruskin, especially after Patmore's conversion, appeared rather to defend himself against his criticism with a gentle irony, as when he promised to show in his writing "something of Catholic Faith wider than yours." But he was as good a friend to Patmore as to his Pre-Raphaelites, and when the first part of *The Angel in the House* appeared he wrote: "I cannot tell you how much I admire your book. I had no idea you had power of this high kind. I think it will, at all events it ought to become, one of the most popular books in the language—and *blessedly* popular, doing good wherever read." He later wrote a long letter to *The Critic*, defending and praising the poem, which had been unfavourably reviewed in that paper. This letter concluded: "Whatever on this head may be the final judgment of the public, I am bound, for my own part, to express my obligations to Mr. Patmore, as one of my severest models and tutors in use of English, and my respect for him as one of the truest and tenderest thinkers who have ever illustrated the most important, because commonest, states of noble human life."

For his part, Patmore reviewed and praised the first volume of *The Stones of Venice* in the *Edinburgh Review*, gaining a letter of thanks from Ruskin's father, who assured him that he had sent the notice on to his son, who was working in Venice on the second volume. Ruskin himself referred to a summary of the first chapter which Patmore had made as "magnificent," adding, "I should like to substitute it in the book itself." In another letter Ruskin gave his opinion of Spanish painters—"a thoroughly irreligious rascally set." This illustrates the division between himself as a thinker and Patmore, who was later to find the Spanish religious temperament the most congenial of all to him.

Other of Ruskin's letters show the efforts he made, on Patmore's initiative, to find patrons and purchasers for the Pre-Raphaelites. There is also a shrewd criticism of Millais: "He has the highest dramatic power—I doubt his reflective faculty."

As Patmore's independence increased in later life, he more often disagreed with Ruskin than Ruskin with him. "You made me very happy, not by disagreeing with me, but by giving me knowledge," Ruskin then wrote. "My belief is that our opinions are—on all subjects with which we are equally acquainted, far more at one than our feelings—closely as these often correspond."

Where Patmore came most to disagree with Ruskin was over the pathetic fallacy. "A description by Wordsworth, Coleridge, or Burns," he wrote, "a landscape by Crome, Gainsborough or Constable, is not merely nature, but nature reflected in and giving expression to a true state of mind. The state of mind is the true subject, the natural phenomena the terms in which it is uttered; and there has never been a greater critical fallacy than that contained in Mr. Ruskin's strictures on the 'pathetic fallacy.' Nature has no beauty or pathos (using the term in its widest sense) but that with which the mind invests it. Without the imaginative eye it is like a flower in the dark, which is only beautiful as having in it a power of reflecting the colours of the light. The true light of nature is the human eye; and if the light of the human eye is darkness, as it is in those who see nothing but surfaces, how great is that darkness!"

When staying with Ruskin in 1875 and 1879 Patmore had many discussions, and once wrote home that Ruskin "is very fond of talking about the Catholic Religion, and says he thinks it likely he shall become a Catholic some day—but I think it is attractive to him only from the idea of pleasant intellectual repose which it presents to him. The arguments for its truth strike him just for the moment, but leave no impression as far as I can see."

The interchanges between Ruskin and Patmore suggest a contrast of temperament and community of interest which made for teasing arguments. With Carlyle it was different. Patmore wrote in the 'seventies when he was "constantly" going to see Carlyle: "The union of our likes and dislikes is quite funny." On another occasion Patmore wrote that
B*

Carlyle was "quite affectionate, he complaining, two or three times, that I had not been to see him lately, and urging me to write, almost as vehemently as he would recommend most of his literary acquaintance—not to do so."

Patmore also commented: "I was a good listener, and never thought of contradicting him, any more than I should have thought of contradicting a locomotive at full speed. I was surprised to find how very few people he saw, though he appeared to be far from difficult of access. There was seldom anybody with him when I spent my evenings at the house."

Carlyle was early an admirer of Patmore's verse, though his highest praise was to tell him that a man with a mind as good as his should rise to the seriousness of prose. Already in 1855 Carlyle wrote: ". . . truly I could not but perceive *good* talent there; —and regret in my heretical way, that you did not strike boldly with it into the rough field of Fact (getting so dreadfully rough, and even hideous and horrid, for want of the like of you so long)."

Five years later Carlyle went further: "The question whether it had not been better that a man of your powers had trained himself to *prose* as exquisitely as you have to verse, and stood by the rigorous *fact* as the gods have unalterably made it, instead of floating, in this light beautiful way, rods and miles above it; the question whether, even in verse itself, with this admirable power of execution, you should not now take some more robust class of subjects, and close the *Troubadour* Enterprise as well finished—these and other questions are still open with me (and I hint them to you at a venture, and because you are no common object to me, nor to the world's interest in this time): but the above truth is beyond question with me, That I spent such an evening over your Book as I have not had for a long time from any other."

Before this reference to *The Angel in the House,* Carlyle had written consolingly on its first reception, scorning the *Plebs* which had become "a sovereign Rhadamanthus of Books." There was hope, because "it is certain, if there *is* any perennial running Brook, were it the smallest rill coming from the eternal fountains, whole Atlantic Oceans of froth will *not* be able to cover it up for ever; said rill will, one day, be *seen* running under the light of the sun, said froth having altogether vanished no man knows whither. That is the law of Nature, in spite of all blustering of any *Plebs* or Devil; and we must silently trust in that."

From this brief examination of Patmore's relations with Ruskin and with Carlyle it emerges that he and Ruskin agreed chiefly on art and differed chiefly on religion, in which the influence exerted was rather by Patmore than Ruskin, who failed to keep him from Rome and was a little attracted in that direction himself; while Carlyle's chief desire was to turn Patmore from verse to prose, in which he had no very evident success, for he had already died when Patmore turned most to prose criticism, though it is possible that Carlyle's respect for his clear-headedness remained an encouragement to him in this.

Indeed, Patmore's independence partly arose from the fact that he was uninfluenced by his contemporaries; his real masters were Coleridge, Plato, the Fathers and Aquinas, to the reading of whom he increasingly turned. It is true that he shared certain ideas with Ruskin and the Pre-Raphaelites, but these were characteristic of the age and a natural development of romanticism. Their common ancestry from Scott and Wordsworth was more important than the fraternal influences inside the movement. Patmore yielded to none of his contemporaries in veneration for Wordsworth, and it was this more than the influence of Ruskin which led him to share their views on art.

Of the Patmores' other visitors it was Tennyson who had most influence on Patmore's poetry, and they were also very close friends in the years immediately before and after Patmore's marriage, and even after Tennyson's own marriage. Patmore had the fervent admiration of a young man for the poetry of Tennyson, who was fourteen years older than himself. When staying with Tennyson he wrote to his wife to say that he was quite content to sit at his feet, as he recognised in him a nature higher than his own.

This friendship and its ending has an interest because it reflects a popular misconception of the relationship between the two men. Even more than most poets, Patmore was deeply immersed in the technique of verse, a subject which he discussed with men as different as Tennyson and Gerard Hopkins. He could not help being impressed by Tennyson's mastery and so was for a time content to be his disciple, as he has often since been regarded.

Yet in reality it would not be easy to find two poets more opposed. With Patmore the subject was everything; he was constantly searching for inspiration and metres to embody the thought which was already perfectly clear in his own head, while Tennyson was searching for subjects on which to employ his own flowing lyrical impulse. It is difficult to appreciate Patmore without some sympathy for his thoughts and feelings, while there is a similar difficulty in failing to appreciate Tennyson, whatever repugnance is aroused by the atmosphere of his work.

But if they were a contrast as poets, they shared certain traits of character, which stimulated their friendship when Patmore was young enough to admire qualities still latent in himself, and disrupted it when his own character had developed the force of Tennyson's. For both stood in front of their fires, airing their views; both were masters; both were independents; but while Tennyson, with his frantic smoking, his nervous depressions and walks at night, was independent in his personal habits, Patmore's independence was of the mind: he would religiously obey the conventions, but refused to conform to the views of his age. Once he could no longer sit at Tennyson's feet, he could no longer stand being in the same room with him.

Yet while it lasted the friendship was close, and afterwards there was always some embarrassment, as occurs when friends at school meet in later life, separated even more by the memory of youth shared than by the years between.

At the time when Patmore was still youthfully looking up to Tennyson, there were already a group of young painters looking up to him, those who had formed the Pre-Raphaelite Brotherhood, united in their devotion to Nature and their mediaeval love of detail. Woolner, the sculptor, the first to become acquainted with Patmore, remained a friend for life. Rossetti showed him drawings and manuscripts, and wrote in a letter to him, "The best one can hope as a painter just now is to have a place of some kind among those who are to do for painting, as far as possible, what you and a very few more poets are doing now for poetry." Sending some of his verse translations to Patmore in 1857, Rossetti wrote and underlined the following words: "Pray remember that all notes or suggested alterations of any kind whatever from you, will be most thankfully received in the margin."

There is an odd note in a letter from Rossetti written in the same year, seven years before Patmore's conversion to Rome, referring to one who "has become a seceder to Roman Catholicism, and is (of course) in consequence a furious admirer of yours." This shows how early such sympathies had developed in Patmore, and it is probable that they would have led to action sooner, if it had not been for his wife's strongly anti-Papist feelings.

In an essay on Rossetti, written many years later, Patmore described him as "thoroughly Italian" in appearance and manners, adding that "in his youth especially he had the sweet and easy courtesy peculiar to his nation."

Later in life Patmore tried to renew his friendship both with Rossetti and with Tennyson, to whom he wrote a long letter which only received a brief acknowledgement. Yet Tennyson's son recorded that his father always wondered why Patmore had "given him up." It was a natural enough development, but it is noteworthy that Patmore took the initiative, for he has sometimes been viewed, owing to the independence and intransigence of his opinions, as a man no less difficult than his friend Carlyle; perhaps both of them occupied a platform to which others were not inclined to climb the steps.

Of all the Pre-Raphaelites, Patmore had least sympathy for Millais, who even as a young man showed some of the qualities to be expected in a future President of the Royal Academy. Yet Patmore spoke tolerantly of his delight in money and honours as "boyish," and it was to Patmore that Millais came asking him to approach Ruskin, when *The Times* made its bitter attack on his work. Ruskin, to whom Patmore at once appealed, wrote his famous letter to *The Times*, which established the Pre-Raphaelites in public respect, for he was already the arbiter of artistic judgment. Patmore had followed the generous tradition of his father, and with even greater effect. Millais had already served Patmore's reputation by the picture based on his poem "The Woodman's Daughter."

Patmore was most attracted, among the Pre-Raphaelites, to Holman Hunt. They had in common a certain simplicity of which they were not ashamed, and an almost primitive sense of religion, rare in the nineteenth century, which led them to treat religious subjects with a natural ease and sincerity that shocked some and made others smile. Holman Hunt's patience in working on "The Light of the World," which took him so long because he refused to paint except in moonlight to catch the authentic shades, or his journey to the Holy Land to paint "The Scapegoat"—these were forms of devotion, at once difficult and simple, likely to appeal intensely to Patmore, who practised the same qualities in his own verse.

On the occasion of Ruskin's letter to *The Times,* Hunt wrote to Patmore, "I am delighted to hear that Ruskin has taken the field in defence of Millais and myself, for I had almost despaired of overcoming the violent opposition to our style which the example of the 'Times' and other influential papers was breeding."

It was Patmore who gave the Pre-Raphaelites most encouragement in their love of detail. He even invented a dictum for them which they accepted with great earnestness: "It is the last rub which gives a polish to the mirror." This care over detail was especially dear to Holman Hunt, who most triumphantly exhibited it in the brambles and burdocks, illuminated by the lamp, on the left of "The Light of the World."

When Hunt was in Jerusalem, preparing for work on "The Scapegoat," he wrote to Patmore, "This blue sky, this hot sun, and the graceful mountains make me rejoice as with new wine, and deafen me to all that comes merely to my outer ears. Yet there is din enough in the world, and truly more than enough to leave one for long in such a mood; and to be honest I must confess my peace is only a sort of intoxication which I caught to escape the great confusion. I wonder whether you try your skill at this riddle—whether it is the same riddle to all, or a different one to each. Shall we take it to pieces? or give it up and wait the sequel? or each work according to our best interpretation to an end?

Why do we live so darkly? work and think so vainly? There is a key to all God's secrets, given to make His servants privy to His course; and yet we know nothing, perhaps because we believe nothing; for truly I think the world has come to this. I see myself always intending, hoping to believe and do; but always excuse myself for the present: and thus I find all others. There is nothing serious in the world—Religion, Politics, and—yes—even War, are only played at."

A month later Hunt wrote to let Patmore into the real secret of his visit to Jerusalem: "As a year will go by before it will be exhibited, I must not let the subject get very well known, but I will tell to you—as no great favour of course—for I should not be surprised if you have already heard—that the picture on which I have been working of late is the 'Scapegoat'—with the background painted from the Dead Sea at Sodom, if the name of Oosdoom, to the further end of the sea, identifies the place."

In the same letter Hunt revealed that natural British sympathy with the Moslems which so long smoothed British progress in the Middle East and in India. Patmore himself was a warm supporter of the Turks. "The Arabs," wrote Hunt, "in principle are much better Christians than either the Greeks or Latins . . . the Holy Sepulchre being a chamber of imagery crammed full of trumpery pictures of old saints, and decorated throughout in that bad taste which Roman Catholics have all to themselves in Europe, but which here the modern Greeks share with them—while the mosques were so free from any offensive feature that they might serve at once for the purest Christian form of worship."

Patmore would hardly have quarrelled with these sentiments even after he had become a Roman Catholic himself, for while his religion was intensely human and anti-puritan, his principles in art always remained austere. He disliked the gauds and tinsel of Continental churches. He had a Pre-Raphaelite preference for simplicity.

In essence perhaps Patmore was more of a Pre-Raphaelite than any of the painters, for one idea runs through all his work, through his poems and through his religion, the idea that truth is to be found only in simplicity, that the only real knowledge is to know more deeply what one already knows. The mediaeval mystic, concentrating on a single mystery of faith, to the exclusion of all other knowledge, was to him the type of the thinker. "All reasoning," he wrote, "ends in an appeal to self-evidence." The direct and instinctive vision of the heart, first revealed in childhood, was the mirror of truth. It was the simplicity of Patmore's verse which first drew the allegiance of the Pre-Raphaelites, for he was a poet always seeking out the commonplace, flowers, birds, trees. He admired the sea because it is deep and simple—the truth of love is like the sea "for clearness and for mystery." For him the clear and the simple were always the mysterious.

This value which he set on simplicity led him to say things which far less intelligent men would not have considered worth saying, just as critics in *The Times* regarded Pre-Raphaelite subjects as unworthy of the dignity of paint. Patmore was not an original thinker or poet in the sense that he uncovered new territories, but in everything he went back to origins, to basic things. Many of his ideas have long been familiar, but forgotten, taken for granted, or dismissed as obvious, yet he sometimes succeeded in making them less obvious than clear and sharp as the dawn. His was the prophetic gift of breathing inspiration into commonplaces, recalling ancient truths to people "whoring after strange gods."

It was a similar moral earnestness in Holman Hunt's character, no less than his painting, which drew Patmore's regard, for there always remained with him a respect for that quality which stood so high in North London intellectual circles. It is one of the amiable traits in Patmore that he retained this respect even when he moved into a very different moral atmosphere and became aware of its perils, even when he said that most of our troubles spring from "a few fools having the courage of their convictions." He was never led into that too facile irony which some Catholics show for ideals which, however narrow or limited, have a real moral fervour behind them. Arthur Waugh once wrote that a lack of humour was typical of Patmore's verse. Perhaps, though it is also a trait of most serious poetry; but it was certainly not typical of his character. He had a truculent sort of humour, the sort that exaggerates, and he relished stories against himself and against his Church, which he characteristically treated as if it was a part of himself, saying that "no one is thoroughly convinced of the truth of his religion who is afraid to joke about it."

Patmore had humour, but he was never ironical at the expense of the moral and intellectual circles he outgrew, whose great idol was Emerson. In an essay on Emerson, Patmore remarked on the "singular force" with which he presented thoughts which "an immense number of the young, intelligent, and sincere of the past and present generation" had tried to follow. Emerson's, he said, "was a sweet and uniformly sunny spirit." The only lighter touch he allowed himself was to say that Emerson disarmed criticism in the same way as the girl who gushed, "Oh, my religion is the religion of the Sermon on the Mount."

Such remarks, which blandly ignore the centuries in which men have struggled to practise that religion, were a commonplace in North London intellectual circles. It is natural that statements not very different appear in Patmore's own earlier work; what is more surprising is his subtlety and

his constant awareness of deeper mysteries. His moral earnestness is sometimes as obvious as Emerson's or Holman
Hunt's. He had the same simplicity, and it is in this that
he is open to the charge of lacking humour. Some of his
verses are easy to laugh at, as out-of-date fashions always are.
He himself called one line of his—"A gift of wine to Widow
Neale"—"the one famous line I have ever succeeded in
writing," so much was it ridiculed. There were others:

> And someone in the Study play'd
> The Wedding-March of Mendelssohn.

But many of these prosaic lines in *The Angel of the House*
usefully balance the more exalted ones:

> I stood by Honor and the Dean,
> They seated in the London train. . . .

Patmore comes down to earth very frequently, but that
was his intention. He even believed that religion had no
power until it had come down to earth.

Other lines, absurd out of their context, only state a simple
fact as simply as possible:

> To breakfast with the Dean at nine

or

> Announced me, "Mr. Felix, Miss."

In this simplicity Patmore was a natural ally of the Pre-
Raphaelite Brotherhood.

The Brotherhood broke up and went their different ways.
It was perhaps Patmore, although he later claimed to be quite
detached from the movement, who followed the most central
path. Chesterton once said of Ruskin, the Pre-Raphaelites'
champion, that he seemed to want every part of the cathedral
except the altar. It was towards the altar that Patmore went.
In so far as the Pre-Raphaelites looked back to the Middle

Ages, issuing from the Gothic revival, the Oxford Movement and the Romantics, having an evident ancestry from Sir Walter Scott and the revival of ballads, Patmore was most true to their principles though, as was his habit, he exaggerated them or at least took them to their furthest point. He always went back as far as he could. In his religion he went back beyond the Church into paganism and even into the most primitive rites, to find there prefigurings of Christian beliefs. In going back beyond Raphael, the Pre-Raphaelites, as their name implied, were reacting against the Renaissance; not content with that, Patmore reacted against the Reformation as well, for even in his early married life he had already begun to read Catholic theology.

No less than Newman, he abhorred compromise. It was logical that Newman should pass out of the Oxford movement, which aimed at a compromise between the established and the mediaeval Church. While both he and Patmore appeared to be isolated in nineteenth-century England and to resist the contemporary current of ideas, a longer perspective shows them as following at least one current to its natural conclusion. For if the eighteenth century had been convinced that the mediaeval and Gothic ages were barbarous and had consistently set classical standards of architecture and literature above them, it was largely because scepticism had rejected religion and preferred the philosophies of the early Roman empire. Gibbon, who was an incarnation of the eighteenth century, declared that the best time to live had been between the death of Domitian and the accession of Commodus. All the movements of the early nineteenth century, from which the Pre-Raphaelites stemmed, turned away from these eighteenth-century ideas and were filled with a nostalgia for the Middle Ages, which the previous generations had despised. Just as scepticism had been the motive of Gibbon, so religion was the impulse behind the new ideas.

Ruskin, in his letter to *The Times* championing the Pre-Raphaelites, had been right to add a warning against the Romanist tendencies among them. It was Patmore, never a member of the Brotherhood, who went over to Rome, and only later, long after it had been dissolved. Yet in this he remained true to the basic Pre-Raphaelite principle, for a man who really went back to an age before Raphael could hardly avoid finding himself inside a church, especially if he was an artist, as there were not many other places where he could use his brush.

Patmore always acted with such independence that he himself never realised the part that the Brotherhood had played in his life. It belonged to the reign of his first wife, while his journey to Rome and his conversion came under his second; but the link is apparent to anyone looking at the chain of circumstances from outside.

Possibly it was the fact that he had acted alone which led him to disregard the association. But it is more likely that he was influenced by his dislike for the style into which Pre-Raphaelite art later developed. One of his dominating ideas was the necessary unity of any work of art; he was firmly against useless decoration and superfluities. He held strong opinions on architecture which earned the respect of the architect, Basil Champneys, who was to become his biographer. Picturesque additions to an old house, Patmore wrote, were nearly always the outcome of some necessity discovered after the first building of it. To copy them in a nineteenth-century building was "mere imbecility aping the movements of reason."

Patmore found a lack of simplicity in the archaic flourishes and repetitions which Rossetti and Morris introduced into their verse. The fact that Rossetti came to be viewed as the central character of the Brotherhood and that he not only "merged" but, as Patmore said, "confounded" the functions of painter and poet, had its counterpart in the movement as a whole, which was so often literary in its inspiration, yet was chiefly represented by painters. The result was poems that painted a picture and pictures that told a story. Both have been and are admired—a group of conservative intellectuals today have almost formed a Pre-Impressionist Brotherhood, fervent as the Pre-Raphaelites, in their enthusiasm for this art—but to Patmore it was a weakness in Rossetti that he scattered in his verse sharply outlined images which interfered with "the natural and truly poetical expression of feeling." Patmore added that "in Rossetti, as in several other modern poets of great reputation, we are constantly being pulled up, in the professedly fiery course of a tale of passion, to observe the moss on a rock or the note of a chaffinch."

This "natural expression of feeling" was one of Patmore's great principles: he refused to write unless he felt strongly. This in itself was enough to place him apart from the Pre-Raphaelites, who were often led into artificiality by their choice of historical or religious subjects for which they lacked depth of feeling. It is significant that when Patmore embarked on his long narrative poem, *The Angel in the House,* he set it in his own day. He followed the principles which he advocated, for it is here and now that a man's strongest feelings are aroused.

But before *The Angel* he published one poem in which traces of Pre-Raphaelite influence are to be found, the first that he had brought out since the early poems, only issued through his father's intervention and afterwards regretted by Patmore himself. This was "Tamerton Church Tower," which appeared in 1853, when he had been seeing most of the Pre-Raphaelites. In this the imagery is less subdued to the theme than in his later work, a fault with which he reproached Rossetti. Perhaps the weakness of the plot, that of contrast between idyllic love and the drowning of the young bride, is partly responsible for this. The poem already has the fluency of *The Angel in the House,* but it is chiefly memorable for such pictures as:

> Our English skies contain'd, that Spring,
> A Caribbean sun;
> The singing birds forgot to sing,
> The rivulets to run.

And:

> But never, when the tide drew back,
> Trod I the weltering strand;
> For horribly my single track
> Pursued me in the sand.

Such gleams stand out against the dull background. The poem flows easily enough, but it lacks the passion which gives a characteristic vehemence to Patmore's later work. Nor had he solved the problem of how to incorporate his philosophical asides, which in *The Angel* take the form of Preludes to each Canto, and in *The Unknown Eros* are fused so wholly into the theme of the ode that philosophy and narrative are one. In "Tamerton Church Tower" one such aside is put into a lover's song:

> When Love's bright Ichor fills the veins,
> Love's Amaranth lights the brow,
> The Past grows dark, the Future wanes,
> Before the golden Now.

In 1853, the year of "Tamerton Church Tower," Patmore had been married six years and his wife had borne him three children, Milnes, the godson of Monckton Milnes, Tennyson, the godson of the poet, and Emily Honoria, named after her mother—Honoria being the name selected for her portrait in *The Angel*. This Emily Honoria was perhaps the most gifted of his children, certainly the one closest to him. All three children were drawn by the Pre-Raphaelites, Milnes by Millais, Tennyson by Holman Hunt, Emily by John Brett.

Their mother, Emily Patmore, was to bear three more children, before she was finally condemned to consumption. In the years of her married life, she not only managed the household and the children, provided calm as well as happiness for her husband, wrote stories and rhymes for children under the name of "Mrs. Motherly," composed a book on domestic arts, helped Patmore to compile *A Children's Garland from the Best Poets,* but also acted as hostess to men who were to become the leading writers and artists of the period. It is a formidable achievement, yet she herself seems to have taken most pride in being the inspirer, collaborator and helper of what she and her husband believed was to be his greatest work, an epic of married love. In their North London household this was as constantly in their thoughts as the prospect of a rise in salary or a move to a larger house are in the minds of other young suburban households. But it was much more than that, for it was also the love and joy they had received, made permanent in verse.

Patmore called his great poem *The Angel in the House.* It has been suggested by those who have a dislike of obvious facts that Patmore was too much of a theologian to identify a woman with an angel. But it is quite certain that he did so—he even referred to his first love as his first "angel"—and it was entirely characteristic of him, as it was of the seventeenth-century tradition of hyperbole to which he looked back. Lovers who identified Heaven with a woman's eye-ball were hardly likely to have scruples with angels. Emily Honoria Patmore and the "Angel in the House" were one and the same person.

Patmore told her that the poem was more hers than his.

IV

Verse at Home

It was not only love, nor even modesty, which led Patmore to ascribe *The Angel in the House* to his wife. She provided both the body and the soul of it, making it possible for him to work and inspiring its whole theme. More than this, it is the sort of achievement that could only have arisen out of the lives of a young and happily married couple.

The Angel is the fruit of Patmore's first life, which was sharply divided from his second and third phases. The seeds of his future development were already planted in it, but Emily Patmore, the perfect wife, was like one sort of English spring, vigorous and stimulating, yet discouraging to the growth of certain flowers and plants, which wait for warmer days.

It is true that she inspired the finest odes in *The Unknown Eros,* written after she had died, but she inspired them only by her death. When he was in the wilderness, which seems to be necessary to the growth of every sort of greatness, to a politician no less than to a poet, he found new resources in himself. The loss of his wife was his greatest tragedy, but it was one which aroused deeper passions than those she had inspired in *The Angel in the House.*

This poem has in it a physical and moral comfort such as she provided in his daily life. She soothed and to some extent suppressed some of his most characteristic impulses. She had been alarmed by the Catholic trend of his thought

47

and had taken upon herself the answering of points raised by such Catholic friends as Aubrey de Vere. Sensing his future development, she said shortly before her death that "they"—the Romanists—would get him when she had gone. That was a prophetic utterance, but her departure opened the way to other experiences than the journey to Rome. There is little doubt that she had given him happiness as perfect as is to be found in an earthly paradise; it was not simply the joy of youth, but the deep satisfaction which only comes from total and daily sharing and understanding. To this was added the vocational fulfilment which is the other form of intense happiness: even when he was seventeen he had decided that he was to be "the poet of marriage," and he could only follow that vocation in the experience of marriage. Emily Patmore gave him all that he desired.

These were the limits which her great qualities imposed, the limits of good fortune, which Balzac once called "the god of fools." There is something of that folly in *The Angel in the House*. The first title projected for it was "The Happy Wedding," one typical of Patmore's peculiar blend of naïveté and defiance. He was never afraid of the commonplace; it was even one of his merits in an age which erred towards grandiloquence. It was not that he was unaware of what was banal; he was too intelligent for that, but his defiance led him to emphasize it, and he wooed the commonplace as ardently as others sought out the exotic. A modern French writer, Raymond Radiguet, who surprised an age of experiment by producing two classical novels before dying in his early twenties, said that every original writer ought to make "a constant effort of banality." Patmore's banality, if not an effort, was at least entirely deliberate. "The Happy Wedding" suggests that easy talk of "a happy marriage" which freezes a couple into a honeymoon for life, concealing all the sacrifices and more poignant joys of which an authentic marriage is constructed. *The Angel in the House*, the title finally decided, has the perfume of other illusions remote from the kitchen sink. Yet, when all the smiles have faded, women themselves may not have been much worse off when they were idealised as angels than when they are lectured as housewives by governments no less resolved than poets to put them in their place.

Once the criticism has been made that *The Angel* contains a little too much of the sort of happiness that, when encountered in a couple, recalls the saying that love may sometimes be no more than "an egoism shared between two," the poem nevertheless reveals deep perceptions, especially in single phrases of the Preludes, subtle in their feminine psychology. Patmore observes, for instance, that a woman's "care to please with pleasing comes" and that she is "drawn herself by what she attracts."

Then again:

> The beauty in her Lover's eyes
> Was admiration of her own.

And:

> Kind souls, you wonder why, love you,
> When you, you wonder why, love none.
> We love, Fool, for the good we do,
> Not that which unto us is done.

Patmore also has a felicity in stating more obvious truths:

> What seems to us for us is true.
> The planet has no proper light,
> And yet, when Venus is in view,
> No primal star is half so bright.

And:

> Be not amazed at life; 'tis still
> The mode of God with His elect

>   Their hopes exactly to fulfil,
>   In times and ways they least expect.

Two more quotations mark the distinction, which meant so much to Patmore, between light loves and marriage:

>   The bliss which woman's charms bespeak,
>   I've sought in many, found in none!
>   In many 'tis in vain you seek
>   What can be found in only one.

And:

>   I vow'd unvarying faith, and she,
>   To whom in full I pay that vow,
>   Rewards me with variety
>   Which men who change can never know.

The Preludes, from which these lines are quoted, introduce each Canto of *The Angel in the House*, which narrates the love, courtship, and marriage of Felix with his Honoria, one of the three daughters of Dean Churchill, living in the Cathedral close at Salisbury. The first three parts of the poem, "The Betrothal," "The Espousals," and "Faithful for Ever," were published between 1854 and 1860. A fourth part, "The Victories of Love," which tells in the form of letters the consolation of Frederick, Honoria's rejected suitor, in his Jane, was not published until 1863, a year after the death of Emily Patmore, and it is in every sense less happy than the earlier parts.

It has been said that *The Angel* is not much read today, but it is eminently readable, almost too readable to a modern taste, for it has a fluency which risks becoming insipid; even at the time there were some who found the octosyllabic quatrains a little tedious. Yet, as Valéry Larbaud well says, they run as easily as a stream and the rhymes are clear as bells. Browning said that *"The Angel* should be the most popular poem that ever was," and Tennyson declared that the women ought to erect a statue to Patmore.

Against this, when Alice Meynell later tried to make George Meredith share her enthusiasm for Patmore, he criticized the Dean's "elastic portliness, as one of the superior police of the English middle class, for whom attendant seraphs in a visible far distance hold the ladder, not undeserved, when a cheerful digestion shall have ceased." Meredith's complex sophistication was at the opposite pole from Patmore's simplicity, though he might have been expected to admire some of the epigrams in *The Angel*, if he had not replaced Patmore in Alice Meynell's friendship.

Yet today just the things which jarred Meredith, too close to the period of the poem, have the charm, though not the humour, which attaches to Trollope. *The Angel* is an evocation of Victorian domesticity, at its most bland, in a Cathedral close in Trollope's own Barchester. Without a sympathy for this, the narrative will not be appreciated; even so, the Preludes retain their intelligence. There is "The Married Lover" with its un-Victorian reminder that "She's not and never can be mine," for in stressing the quieter feminine virtues Patmore only emphasized more strongly the dignity of woman; as he noted later, men preach but women set the example. In the narrative, too, there are breaths of spring, as when he so happily intertwines the refrain of the *Pervigilium Veneris* in his verse:

> When like to like is gladly moved,
>   And each thing joins in Spring's refrain,
> "Let those love now who never loved;
>   Let those who have loved love again."

The fluency of Patmore's verse is only surpassed by the poet most opposed to him in temperament and outlook,

Byron. *The Angel* has the fluency of *Don Juan,* though Patmore lacked the facility of Byron, who often composed and memorised whole stanzas while out riding. Patmore's verses have more the air of being composed while pacing up and down a Victorian drawing-room.

There are also unexpected relations in his poems, for it is one of the surprises inherent in the angularity of his character that, while he was to be a friend of Hopkins and, in his later poems, *The Unknown Eros,* wrote in a style more representative of the twentieth century than the staid eighteen-fifties, his *Angel* had in it exaggerated simplicities which looked back to Crabbe even more than to Wordsworth, while its theme and development appealed so much to the most bourgeois of Victorians that it eventually became a best-seller. Nor is it difficult to detect in it lines as sublimely ridiculous as Wordsworth's famous opening to a sonnet, "Jones, while from Calais southward you and I. . . ."

Some lines even have a charm in their absurdity:

> Dear Saint, I'm still at High-Hurst Park.
> The house is fill'd with folks of mark.

Or:

> And Major-domo, Mrs. Rouse,
> A dear old soul from Wilton House.

Such lines show how well-adapted these metres were to the lighter use that was made of them by Belloc. But some are themselves light, as when Felix has just finished a letter to Honoria when he receives one from her:

> I ended. "From your Sweet-Heart, Sir,"
>   Said Nurse, "The Dean's Man brings it down."
> I could have kiss'd both him and her.
>   "Nurse give him that, with half-a-crown."

There is also a relation with Tennyson, but it is excessive to treat Patmore only as a minor Tennyson, for such comparisons, superficial as those which describe a city with canals as a minor Venice, become ludicrous when they associate men who grew so far apart, whose work was such a contrast in atmosphere and in temperament. Tennyson may be the most melodious of all English poets, yet even those most moved by the music of his verse would hardly deny that he was a representative Victorian, the Queen's poet laureate in fact and in reality. It is true that Patmore's name also came up for the same position, when Gladstone was reported to have said, "Patmore died long ago," unwilling to admit that others could share his own legendary powers of survival. But even as a poet Patmore stood significantly alone in his age in that he hardly wrote anything but love poetry—and it is this fact, the material and the emotional content of his verse, rather than its quality, high though some of it is, which sets him apart, for in this he renewed a tradition of English literature which had been in abeyance since the seventeenth century: there had been love lyrics certainly, but there had not been love poets, in the sense that Herrick and Lovelace were poets of earthly, Herbert and Vaughan poets of spiritual love, and Donne of both.

Time had passed. What once seemed a sacred fire and the natural expression of passion, to the nineteenth century seemed rather an indecent sentimentality, only less shocking when applied to love in the home than when it rose to chant the spirit's passion for the uncreated love. "A power not ourselves making for righteousness," or other chill phrases which described an unknown god, were unlikely to inspire odes of religious passion; nor were those written in an earlier tradition likely to be appreciated in such an atmosphere.

Yet something remained. The lively passions of the seventeenth century in which human and divine love spoke the same language, itself both human and divine, were no longer felt in the eighteenth century, when the same scepticism was applied to enduring emotion as to institutions which claimed permanence; but the romantic revival at the beginning of the nineteenth century had its own spiritual passions, superficially religious in a Chateaubriand, deeper in a Manzoni and in the swell of emotion which prompted the Oxford Movement, but most widely expressed in the insistence on romantic love, in which there was a strong religious element. In particular nineteenth-century England, reacting against the Revolution which it had fought to a standstill and anxious to preserve the social framework of the country, welcomed romantic love, once it had received an English coating of domestic comfort and respectability, because it acted as a stable element in a rapidly changing society. In fiction at least, and increasingly in life, romantic love became the reward of the industrious apprentice and the balcony up which the manufacturer climbed into the country house, no less than the means by which women acquired husbands in classes above or below them. It was romantic, but it was also respectable.

No doubt this was a tradition old as the fairy stories and never entirely abandoned, but the romantic revival gave it a new force which in social life counterbalanced the decline of religion. The ideal of love as sacred and the immense reticence on the subject, as in the innermost shrine of some oriental religion, dominated Victorian society. Women became cloistered beings, almost as in the Moorish tradition of Spain, and their angelic qualities were the theme of many novelists.

When in the middle of the century Coventry Patmore published *The Angel in the House* he seemed to be the natural laureate of this sentiment; and his success was so

great that it has clung around his name ever since, still
obscuring his later and greater achievements.

It is true that *The Angel* embodied many Victorian sentiments—its popularity was sufficient proof of that—and it is
no less true that it was from the same soil that his later work
drew its sustenance. But his later development went far beyond that, into a world quite different from that of his
contemporaries, so that he came to shock those who had most
admired him. Yet it was a development, not a change of
direction: the only true learning, he was fond of repeating,
was to know better what was already known; and that was
the only learning which served him in the transition from
The Angel in the House to *The Unknown Eros*.

This raises the question whether the public which delighted in the first and was unable to follow Patmore in
his later work, had not perhaps mistaken the trend of the
first; and a careful reading of *The Angel in the House*
does in fact reveal considerably more than the ordinary
Victorian idealisation of love, which owed so much to the
romantic movement. For Patmore's early association with
the Pre-Raphaelites and the romantic tone of much in his
verse obscures the fact that his whole cast of mind was the
opposite of romantic; in his critical essays he constantly
attacked "emotional art" and in comparing Crabbe with
Shelley he showed how little he was in sympathy with the
romantic tendency in poetry.

The essential difference between Patmore's view of life
and the Victorian ideal of love lies in this fact that he was
opposed to the romantic exaltation and insisted on the
earthly roots of human affection. He would have approved
Peacock's criticism of romanticism in *Nightmare Abbey:*
"You talk like a Rosicrucian, who will have nothing but a
sylph, who does not believe in the existence of a sylph, and

C

who yet quarrels with the whole universe for not containing a sylph." Like Peacock too, Patmore reacted strongly against the melancholy of romanticism, noting "that the good are gay is a commonplace" and declaring that since the beginning of the century "many of our geniuses have mingled their songs with tears and sighs over 'insoluble problems' and 'mysteries of life' which have no existence for a man who is in his right senses and who minds his own business."

The truculence of this declaration is typical of Patmore: the whole tone of the man is there, the impatience, the insistence that a man should be "in his right senses" and recognise his own limitations. In this, his religious attitude has something in common with Peacock's genial paganism, for both were based on a classical criticism of life which assumed a certain standard of thought and behaviour in the republic of letters.

Romantic neither in his literary opinions nor in his attitude to love, Patmore has yet been considered one of the most exaggerated of Victorian romantics. This may largely be due to a confusion of language by which "romantic" has been applied to any strong sentiment. Patmore's descriptions of women are often high-flown, but they are in the earlier tradition of symbolism in which the human becomes the image of the divine.

That is the essential distinction between Patmore and his contemporaries, that his exalted language was exactly used. When he compared a woman's face to an altar, he was not simply paying her a compliment by presenting an image which had a tradition of respect behind it: he really meant that the sight of her was exalting and aroused religious thoughts. Similar language in Swinburne and even in Rossetti had the opposite intention, to place religious imagery on the level of romantic love; and Swinburne had a further aim of desecration in the most accurate sense, as when he addressed an artist's model as "Our Lady of Pain." Such a remark was not intended as a compliment; it was an ironic gibe.

The contrast with Swinburne, who supplanted Patmore in the public's favour, sets the two attitudes in relief. Swinburne's sumptuous imagery was flung over an idea almost as simple as a well-known painting, "Youth at the Prow and Pleasure at the Helm." Patmore's more commonplace language was devoted to the idea of human love as both a rehearsal and a symbol of divine love. Yet because both poets were enclosed in the boots and waistcoats of their age, both aristocratic by temperament and intensely nationalistic, both with a fire and vehemence which gave a certain strength even to their less inspired verses, these showed a few common traits: the "angel" and the "goddess" braid their hair not so very differently. Yet the ideas remain at opposite poles, though this appears less in their use of images than in the echoes of their verse: Swinburne at his best has a little of the sad beauty and mortal charm of Catullus, while Patmore's memorable lines are nearer, though they are very far from attaining, to the accurate definitions of Horace. This Horatian element in Patmore—he had at least the intensely male accents of Horace—was apparent in the way he looked back to the eighteenth century and upheld Augustan standards of criticism.

Patmore was no romantic, though he was strongly passionate and sensual by nature; this was the most striking feature in his physical composition, as it is the most obvious trait. in portraits of him, no less evident than the humour in the eyes. That was his temperament, but another material fact comes only second in importance, the fact that he was an Englishman of the Victorian age.

For all Patmore's independence, for all his subtlety and brilliance, *The Angel* remains intensely English and Victorian. This is its merit, for such flowers of poetry spring only from their natural soil. To present posterity with the fine flower of English domestic life was also Patmore's avowed intention, to show that, as Greece excelled in "images" and Rome in "laws," so "home and private love" were the great virtues of "that ancient English isle." It is at least true that "home" is a word with uniquely English associations, though the claim that love only soared to the heights in England is perhaps on a level with other claims made by every nation at a time when it is "world champion," by France, by Spain, by America, for it is a part of greatness to offer itself to the world not only as a power, but as a model of virtue. Yet when the element of exaggeration is removed, it remains true that the characteristic English qualities are more often found in private rooms than in the market-place, or in public architecture or statuary.

The Angel does display these domestic felicities, nor is it sufficient criticism to say that it idealises them, for such idealism is the stuff of poetry. It is more cogent to point out that these felicities were given too prosperous and too exceptional a setting, as there are some who would argue that married love owes much to such amenities, and Patmore, who shirked financial details hardly less than Balzac, expressly states that his hero Felix had six hundred a year from his lands, a comfortable sum at that time, and owned a house where Queen Elizabeth I had slept, which though common enough in England is hardly a property enjoyed by the whole population; while the Dean says that Honoria only has three thousand so far, but will have more in due course; and Felix also has expectations, for Honoria's aunt in mocking them uses the classic phrase, "Rich aunts and uncles never die." Felix further considers becoming a Member of Parliament, which in those days was still largely a preserve of the rich. It is also true that Patmore indulged his couple with comforts that had been lacking in his own life and his constant implication is, as he was later to write, that "hereditary honour" creates "a standard of truth and courage."

Yet *The Angel* was planned as a domestic epic, and it is further true that every epic has been based on similar assumptions. Hector and Achilles were the heirs of great families and had treasure besides valour to commend them; neither Ariosto nor Tasso wrote of common men and even Milton's Satan had fallen from great heights. It was the epic tradition, and perhaps there is more force in Gosse's remark that Patmore was better endowed for the writing of lyrics than for the epic. Today the long narrative in verse is in disfavour, though it is puzzling that those who have the patience to sit through a long Victorian novel do not find time for *The Angel*. As a period piece alone it has charms, enhanced by a tenderness and a subtlety which are as permanent as human nature. It is clear as water which only reveals the treasures of its depths to those who explore them.

Osbert Burdett, in *The Idea of Coventry Patmore,* a lucid and comprehensive survey of Patmore's philosophy, devoted half the book to *The Angel,* intending to show that Patmore, as he based his views on marriage rather than love, had a firmer foundation than more abstract thinkers. Certainly *The Angel* is admirably concrete, but in spite of its permanent human truths it is also intensely individual, reflecting not only the period but the idiosyncrasies of the man who wrote it. If it is a weakness in Plato that he assumed the existence of slavery, it is a comparable weakness in Patmore that he required a Cathedral close and a country house where Queen Elizabeth I had slept.

Patmore's Honoria is a completely human being and a wife. Dante's Beatrice was something more, but also for more ordinary purposes something less, than a woman rooted in daily reality. Patmore revealed the detail and the background in which Honoria and her Felix loved and lived, thus making her certainly more concrete than a Beatrice but also narrowing her range as a universal symbol.

Honoria was in fact firmly modelled on the solid virtues of Emily Patmore, who was a daughter of a minister, if not a Dean. This is not to limit her, but simply to place her in her rightful setting. It is also material that Felix shared the prejudices and the ambitions of Patmore himself.

For this reason Burdett's examination of Patmore's philosophy, admirable though it is as a summary of his thought, scattered among his verse and prose, requiring just such a synthesis, is perhaps less useful than an enquiry into his life and thought together, for in few men were these so closely joined. Certainly Patmore's philosophy embodies those universal truths which Burdett claimed to find in it, but they were also embodied in the man himself, and it is by their fruits in him that they must also be judged. A man is more than an idea, as even the founder of a religion is more than a Church. Whatever Patmore was in himself is reflected in his work, both his limitations and his greatness. However high a man's inspiration, it is always something less than his example; the blood of the martyrs is more effective than their teaching, and in the end it is only the lives of the saints which recall people to what they preached.

The Angel shows both the man and his thought, but with Patmore the difference between the two was further complicated by the part played by his wife, both in his life and in his work. One of the difficulties in writing about marriage is that it is a matter of such general experience that most people's views on it are coloured by their own, and they are inclined to consider any statement made on it as simply another individual impression. One attitude to Patmore's exalted conception of marriage may be a shrug of the shoulders and the remark, "Evidently he was happily married," while a cynic may also add, "And three times."

Another form of this criticism is simply to say that *The Angel* is a great tribute to Emily Patmore. This it certainly is, and a tribute such as few women have ever received. In writing of marriage Patmore asked for the gift of saying things "too simple and too sweet for words." This was beyond his, beyond any man's powers, but in writing of Honoria he succeeded better in displaying the graces of Emily Patmore. *The Angel in the House* is her glory. Only a woman of her quality could have sustained Patmore in his belief that "all grace is the grace of God" and encouraged him to sublimate human love:

> The richest realm of all the earth
> Is counted still a heathen land:
> Lo, I, like Joshua, now go forth
> To give it into Israel's hand.

Yet he was perhaps more like Moses than Joshua when he wrote *The Angel*, for he saw the promised land of divine love, but failed to enter it. Earthly ties were still too strong.

"All men are led to Heaven by their own loves," he was later to write, "but these must first be sacrificed."

V

Love and Death

Emily Patmore had been in poor health, and at times seriously ill, for some years, so that eventually the younger children had to be boarded out with friends, but it only became clear in her last year that there was no escape from her death by consumption. She died in the summer of 1862. The prolonged illness had given enough warnings and she had not only prepared calmly for the end, but made arrangements for the children, the youngest of whom was only two, and had even accustomed the older ones to the idea that they would in time have a new mother.

These six children were either at school or staying with friends at the time of her death. Their father, who was still working at the British Museum, went to lodgings, but contrived to see or write to them almost daily.

His grief was proportionate to his devotion and to the joy which had gone out of his life, yet it is characteristic of him that, lonely and unhappy though he was, he consoled himself not by laments, nor by the blankness of melancholy, but by recapitulating and living over again the joys which he and Emily Patmore had shared together. He even went back to Hastings, to the place where they had spent their honeymoon, a return which, he told his eldest daughter, made him both very happy and very sad. But he achieved that happiness which comes from facing grief and is denied those who avoid sadness at all cost. One of his later sayings emphasized the permanence of love and joy that had truly entered the heart, and it was from these accumulated joys that he drew the strength to survive. Even so, he believed that only the fact that the gravity of her illness had gradually prepared him for the idea of her death saved him from a complete breakdown.

One or two of his friends among the Pre-Raphaelites, and Monckton Milnes, the godfather of his eldest child, did what they could to help, while Aubrey de Vere tried to distract him with the project of a journey to Rome. But Tennyson, whose wife had also been a friend of Emily Patmore's, neither visited him, nor wrote. Instead Patmore received a letter from the Royal Literary Fund, offering help, on the initiative of Mr. and Mrs. Tennyson. He took this in bad part and refused the offer. From that moment the breach with Tennyson was never healed, though many years later when Patmore attempted a reconciliation it emerged from Tennyson's brief reply that he had never received a letter which Patmore wrote him at this time, a mischance which explains this particular lapse, though they had been drifting apart for less dramatic reasons before this incident.

In his grief Patmore was greatly burdened with cares for his children, not only emotional but material. Harassed as he was, it was understandable that he should sometimes have been irritable, as also happens to fathers and writers without the excuse of grief. One or two letters written to his children at this time are different from anything that a father would write today, as their references to the mother's death recall certain passages in Dickens, not his happiest, and what the waves said about Paul Dombey, while their exhortations to virtue have been superseded today by a tradition of jocularity towards children which was previously reserved for a particular type of uncle. Whether children are as gratified as parents by the change is less certain, for they

C*

have their own seriousness and their own attitude towards death which, if more "horrible," is not necessarily less healthy or less natural than the silence of their elders. Patmore wrote as a Victorian father, and there may even be fathers today who would write not so very differently in as serious a mood, if they were sure that the letter would not be seen by their sophisticated friends or by professional educators.

In 1863, the year following the loss of his wife, Patmore wrote to his eldest daughter Emily, who bore the name of her dead mother: "Nothing, now, can make me so happy as the knowledge that my little ones are happy. Your new companions must be a great addition to your pleasure. I only hope you do not get so *very* happy as you did at Dorchester. We ought never to get so boisterously happy ourselves as to forget the respect we owe to older people. And *noisy* happiness *is* disrespectful to them."

Toward the end of the same year he wrote: "I am rejoiced to think that you know and feel too thoroughly that the only way to be happy is to be good and true for it to be necessary to say anything about that—except to remind you that the way to be continually *more* happy is to be continually *more* entirely good, and that the only way to be really good is to love Christ. . . .

"I hope that you thank God, at this season, for all the good He has done you. He took away dear Mama, a year and a half ago, because she had grown too good for it to be of any use for her to live longer in this world. That was a terrible misfortune for you; but think how many things God has done towards making up for that evil."

On Boxing Day he wrote: "The presents were received with rapture. Bertha put on her beautiful dress, before we had the Xmas Tree, and Henry embraced his book for two whole hours in a quiet ecstasy.

"I have posted your letter to Milnes. Poor fellow, I fear

he has had a sad Xmas, among his swearing, grog-drinking shipmates. *Next* Xmas, however, he will probably spend with us, and we will make it *so* happy to him, will we not?"

In the following month, January 1864, he wrote gaily, giving news of the other children: "They are all as round and fat as dumplings, and look as bright as a May morning."

Patmore was very much a father, not only in fathering seven children—he had another by his third wife—but in the whole cast of his mind. Paternalism was an element in his philosophy and he was by nature a patriarch. England today is perhaps more used to matriarchs, and there has been corresponding criticism of a past generation of fathers, but such criticism surely went too far when it was apt to suggest that the man who was most aware of his position as a father was less fond of his children than those who are more casual. Patmore loved his children and, with one exception, there is evidence that they loved him. The exception was the eldest child, Milnes.

With two of the other children, Emily and Henry, he was on the closest of terms, and they discussed all their interests and aspirations with him even after they were grown up. Bertha and Gertrude lived happily at home with their mother's successors. The only difficulty was with Milnes; there was none with Tennyson, though he took less readily than the girls and the younger children to his father's second marriage; and it would be unusual to find a family of six in which none of the children reacted against the father.

It is likely that Patmore was both clumsy and impatient with the small children; there is indeed his own confession of his failure, "The Toys," the simplest and most memorable of his poems:

My little Son, who look'd from thoughtful eyes
And moved and spoke in quiet grown-up wise,

Having my law the seventh time disobey'd,
I struck him, and dismiss'd
With hard words and unkiss'd,
His Mother, who was patient, being dead.
Then, fearing lest his grief should hinder sleep,
I visited his bed,
But found him slumbering deep,
With darken'd eyelids, and their lashes yet
From his late sobbing wet.
And I, with moan,
Kissing away his tears, left others of my own;
For, on a table drawn beside his head,
He had put, within his reach,
A box of counters and a red-vein'd stone,
A piece of glass abraded by the beach
And six or seven shells,
A bottle with bluebells
And two French copper coins, ranged there with careful art,
To comfort his sad heart.
So when that night I pray'd
To God, I wept, and said:
Ah, when at last we lie with trancèd breath,
Not vexing Thee in death,
And Thou rememberest of what toys
We made our joys,
How weakly understood
Thy great commanded good,
Then, fatherly not less
Than I whom Thou hast moulded from the clay,
Thou'lt leave Thy wrath, and say,
"I will be sorry for their childishness."

This is the most popular of Patmore's verses, nor are
there any in the language which more accurately reveal the

emotions of a father. They also display that child-like attitude towards God which has recently seemed more native
to Italy than to the austere climate of England. This awareness of men as children put Patmore on a level with his own
and reduced the aloofness of a parent.

An added interest in this most fatherly of poems is that the
son in question was Milnes, the one child who was always
at odds with his father.

As much could be made of the attitude of eldest sons to
their Victorian fathers as has been made of the hostility with
which Princes of Wales have faced the royal Georges. The
future Henry V trying on the crown of his father is a prec-
edent which has found many followers. Just as there comes
a moment when growing daughters sharply differ in taste
from their mothers, so for sons there is a reaction against
fathers, often strongest when the character is most similar.
Milnes, Patmore's eldest son, had this sort of antagonism
towards his father.

It is sometimes argued that the strong hand of a father
produces weakness or timidity in the eldest son. This was
certainly not so with Milnes, whose rebellion arose from high
spirits and a light-hearted attitude towards discipline. He was
early destined to the sea, and his godfather, Monckton
Milnes, who always took a warm interest in him, arranged
for him to become a naval cadet on the *Britannia*. His boisterous spirits did not suffer away from home, but they did
make him refractory to naval discipline. Unfortunately the
most critical period came immediately after his mother's
death. Reports were unsatisfactory. Persistent insubordina-
tion could not be cured by the punishment of night-watches,
which Milnes seemed to enjoy. Captain Powell, in charge of
the cadets, was adamant, and Patmore's efforts to intercede
were unsuccessful. After repeated warnings Milnes had to
leave; he served before the mast on a merchant ship and after

adventures at sea eventually became master of his own ship, his father having found the money for him to buy it.

That is the whole story. It is evident that Patmore suffered from it and from the loss of his son's affection. In the last part of *The Angel,* published after his wife's death, in tracing the career of Frederick, the rejected lover, who also went to sea, he used these words:

> I lay and wept, of dawn afraid,
> And thought, with bursting heart, of one
> Who, from her little, wayward son,
> Required obedience, but above
> Obedience still regarded love.

Both these lines and "The Toys" suggest that he reproached himself for a failure in love towards Milnes, and a father who was really a domestic tyrant would have been more likely to reproach the son.

The problem of Milnes has been emphasized because it is the basis of Patmore's reputation as a stern parent. By later standards there is some truth in the charge, but it was magnified and misrepresented by Joseph Conrad's use of the story in his novel *Chance,* published in 1914, the first of his novels to reach a really wide public.

It is unlikely that Conrad knew the story in any detail. What appealed to him was, in the words of Henry James about his own work, "the stray suggestion, the wandering word, the vague echo, at touch of which the novelist's imagination winces as at the prick of some sharp point."

Unhappily for Patmore's reputation, Conrad was at no pains to disguise the source of his inspiration. Patmore himself does not appear in the book, but he is referred to under the name of Carleon Anthony, as the father of the chief character, Captain Anthony, who is shown as a man thwarted by his father's temper. Carleon Anthony is a poet whose works read "like sentimental novels told in verse" which was "felicitous." The reference to *The Angel in the House* was rendered unmistakable for those acquainted with the poem by a reference to "six thousand years' traditions of civility" at the beginning of the first Canto. Conrad commented in his novel, "Why he fixed the term at six thousand years I don't know." He described Carleon Anthony—Coventry Patmore—as "a savage sentimentalist who had his own decided views of his paternal prerogatives. He was a terror. . . ." The poet was also "a man with a handsome face, arbitrary and exacting with his dependents, but marvellously suave in his manner to admiring strangers." There is also a reference to "his second wife's death," and the sketch concludes with the words that there were "doubts as to Carleon Anthony's complete sanity for some considerable time before he died."

Unlike Patmore in that, Anthony also differed from him in having only two children, the sea-captain and a daughter whose husband was very proud of his wife's parentage and constantly mentions his brother-in-law as "the son of Carleon Anthony, the poet—you know." This is one of the Conrad refrains of the book, comparable to "youth, youth, youth."

Conrad's was only one of the first attempts at what became known as "debunking" the Victorians, later carried out not only in fiction but in biography, or in a skilful blend of the two. A legitimate literary experiment, it achieved some fresh judgments, but also some distortions. Patmore's aloof figure in the Victorian ranks naturally drew the first fire.

The portrait of him in *Chance* is a caricature, but one recognisable not only to those prejudiced against Patmore, who was not popular with Conrad's generation. That it is recognisable indicates that there must have been a grain of truth in it. That Conrad had Patmore in mind is proved by the similarities noted above. It is also relevant that the second most important character in the book is a Captain Powell, the name of the officer who condemned Milnes, and this name is given prominence as it is also that of a shipping master in the book. If Conrad had known all the facts of the story he would surely have avoided taking the name of a real character in it.

The use that Conrad made of such facts as he had is strange. The plot of the book turns on the reluctance of Captain Anthony, "the son of the poet—you know," to consummate his marriage, which is due to the influence of his "sentimental" father. Patmore would have felt the same horror at this implication as he showed when one of his convent-bred daughters said that she thought marriage was "rather a naughty sacrament." He could be more justly accused of sensuality than of sentimentality in such matters.

Milnes too, who was apparently the model of Captain Anthony, was more a boisterous character than a sentimentalist. But *Chance* is an effective novel and Patmore—Carleon Anthony—was necessary to the plot.

As to the grain of truth in the caricature, the strained relations between Patmore and his son Milnes are indisputable; according to the youngest son, the child of the third wife, Milnes remained aloof even at his father's funeral. It is also true that there was a strong patriarchal and authoritative element in Patmore; it is further true that he was a poet. He was certainly handsome, but the portrait of him as "a savage sentimentalist" and "a terror" is more an opinion than a statement of act. That was not the view of his other children, nor of his friends.

In what sense he was sentimental is more difficult to decide, partly owing to the different shades of meaning in the word, particularly in different periods. His friend and biographer, Basil Champneys, writing at the beginning of this century, confessed to a dislike of what he called passages of "the physiologico-sentimental type." This curious phrase seems to refer to such incidents as a mother giving the breast to her child, which another generation might call sensual rather than sentimental. Patmore, like many baroque artists, often failed to distinguish between the sensual and the sentimental; that was both his character and his belief. His senses and feelings ran together. Perhaps that is his chief importance both to our age and to his, both to those who insist on the realism of the senses and to those who insisted on romance. He is an example of the natural and traditional attitude to those who would consult only their doctors about their love affairs, as he was to those who would only consult the poets.

But there are others, beyond poets and doctors, who have a say on the question of marriage; there are the priests and lawgivers of mankind. Perhaps they pressed on Patmore most hardly. It was his senses which were the deepest anguish, as they were the joy, of his life. He was human enough in that: what is more remarkable is his loyalty to his own character. A man of such character who recognises the obligations of morality, whether these are obligations to God or to society, has the choice of suppressing his passions entirely, which involves the two risks of nullity and hypocrisy, or of directing them in such a way that they serve a higher purpose, which involves the risks of ignominious failure or constant frustration. It is not an easy choice, but the only remaining course is a surrender which leads to disintegration of character and a death which, at least to a Christian, can hardly be the release which it may appear to those for whom death is a locked door.

In this dilemma, Patmore lived up to the human ideal of faith until death; but he has been more harshly judged for not living up to a romantic ideal of faith in this world after death, that popular Victorian conception of the husband who devotes the rest of his life to the memory of his dead wife, haunting her grave and perhaps keeping a vase of fresh flowers beneath her portrait in the drawing-room, or leaving her room exactly as it was, locking the door and going there to brood through heart-broken nights. This would have appealed very much to the public which had enjoyed Patmore's *Angel in the House*. It is a romantic ideal, nor is it an ignoble one; but, once more, Patmore was not a romantic. It is also material to the question that his first wife had urged him to remarry and provide their six young children with a mother; and it is a further fact of common human experience that men left with young children do usually marry a second time.

Common human experience is not what the world admires in its poets and its great men, but it is unfortunately true that even the greatest men are not wholly the masters of the experience which life brings to them. They can control their reactions to events, but not the events themselves, whether these are public calamities or the death of those closest to them. Lamartine once said of Balzac that he was a great man to whom the fates had been mean. The fates were perhaps generous to Coventry Patmore in giving him nearly fifteen years of great happiness with his first wife, but in cutting the thread of her life they confronted him at the age of forty-one with a problem which he spent the rest of his life trying to solve.

If it was not for that problem, his life would be robbed of a large part of its interest; and for posterity his fascination lies in the fact that this problem is one which, in some form or other, faces the majority of men once their youth has passed. For it is the experience of a great number of men, as it was his, to base their whole happiness on human love and then in middle life to find that there is some fault in the foundations, even a danger of collapse. This collapse is not always brought about by death, nor even by disillusionment. Sometimes it is no more than the realisation that what in youth seemed eternal is subject to the motion of time, which advances at increasing speed towards death, the agonizing problem of all mankind.

This crisis of middle life is a favourite theme with the novelists, but it has been less considered by the poets who, as Mistral once said, are "always twenty years old." It is true that Patmore preserved some youthful fire in old age and retained the ability to love almost as astonishingly as Goethe; but the crisis came to him and affected his whole future development.

It was less a crisis in his poetry than in his whole attitude to life. His wife's death was not itself the crisis; this shock simply confronted him with the issue which forces men to enquire of what value is human love in a world dominated not only by death but by the more terrible mortality which preys equally on the deepest emotions and strongest convictions of men, unless these rest on foundations outside themselves and their world.

Love, of its nature, when it reaches a certain depth, is forced to consider the problem of death, for there is a permanence in love which refuses to admit its end, as definitely as sanity refuses to accept suicide. Love demands survival. Yet death is always close at hand and the gayest songs insist on this—let us love before perpetual night—gather rosebuds— love is not hereafter: the refrain at least is deathless. Youth itself is haunted by dreams of dead lovers. Yet the dead belong to another world: wherever they are, they are not here; the most complete sceptic admits so much.

Patmore had always been vividly aware of enduring love, but it was the fact that his own love had vanished into another world that compelled him to realise that love's true place always was in the other world. Death was for him the opening rather than the shutting of a door, and the identity of his angel in the house was even more evident to him when she had vanished into the world ordinarily inhabited by angels.

He differed from that long line of poets who have lamented death as the end of love; for him, death was the fulfilment of love, which only had its rehearsal in this life.

Emily Patmore was dead, but he had only to wait to be reconciled with her in the other world. He could look forward to death with the hope that led Browning to write after his wife's death:

> O thou soul of my soul! I shall clasp thee again,
> And with God be the rest!

These two lines of Browning, the last of "Prospice," occur in some editions of his poems immediately before "A Face," the tribute he wrote to Emily Patmore which has been quoted earlier. Browning and Patmore both lost wives they loved deeply, but the two poets and widowers reacted differently: Browning remained faithful to the memory of his wife, while Patmore married again two years and thirteen days after his first wife's death.

Both men were firm believers, assured that they would be reunited with their wives. Both were men of strong passions, tempted to console themselves with other women.

No man is in a position to disentangle the threads of fate and character in a life, to decide what was the result of circumstances, what the result of choice, but more people will probably be attracted by Browning's behaviour in this matter than by Patmore's. It is even possible that Patmore realised this, for though he always spoke of Browning with respect it is remarkable that he did not go out of his way to praise the greatest Christian poet of his day.

Browning himself was always indulgent towards Patmore—
it was he who had from the first prophesied the great popularity which *The Angel in the House* eventually attained.
Later, on the death of Patmore's son Henry, he wrote: "On
any other occasion, I should have felt happy at the opportu-
nity of assuring you that the many years which have gone
by since I first became acquainted with you have in no way
altered my impression of the genius which came on us all by
surprise in your first volume."

To this Patmore replied: "It is long since I have received
any letter giving me so much pleasure as is given me by that
which I have received from you."

Browning certainly showed greater loyalty to his wife than
Patmore to his. But if Browning was more devoted, it is also
possible that he was more fortunate in his marriage. Patmore
had been entirely devoted to his wife, but his religious
development had been shocking to her, and she had known
that it would lead to greater changes after her death. Browning remained the same man after his wife's death, but
Patmore was confronted with a different destiny, one which
was to wreck the unity of his life and work with Emily
Patmore.

He always believed firmly in reunion with her beyond the
grave, yet he clearly sensed, in his grief for his wife's death,
something more than the personal loss, because he embodied
in one of his finest poems—"Departure"— the bewilderment,
the loss of direction, and the break in destiny which this
foreshadowed:

It was not like your great and gracious ways!
Do you, that have nought other to lament,
Never, my Love, repent
Of how, that July afternoon,
You went,

With sudden, unintelligible phrase,
And frighten'd eye,
Upon your journey of so many days,
Without a single kiss, or a good-bye?
I knew, indeed, that you were parting soon;
And so we sate, within the low sun's rays,
You whispering to me, for your voice was weak,
Your harrowing praise.
Well, it was well
To hear you such things speak,
And I could tell
What made your eyes a growing gloom of love,
As a warm South-wind sombres a March grove.
And it was like your great and gracious ways
To turn your talk on daily things, my Dear,
Lifting the luminous, pathetic lash
To let the laughter flash,
Whilst I drew near,
Because you spoke so low that I could scarcely hear.
But all at once to leave me at the last,
More at the wonder than the loss aghast,
With huddled, unintelligible phrase,
And frighten'd eye,
And go your journey of all days
With not one kiss, or a good-bye,
And the only loveless look the look with which you pass'd:
'Twas all unlike your great and gracious ways.

This is so natural and human that it softens the selfishness of which it has been accused. All grief is selfish; if it is not, it becomes pity, not grief. That "you" have gone and left "me" is the essence of grief which contains more than a querulous complaint.

The first result of his wife's death inevitable in a man

of Patmore's temperament, was to intensify his religious life, as he was one of those for whom the point at which love and death intersect is the centre of the universe. Among the papers found at his own death was a reference to God's marriage with humanity, of which the marriage of man and woman was the symbol. "This is the burning heart of the Universe." This last phrase was underlined.

This symbolic relation between divine and human love, which was to become the basis of all his thought, had already been prefigured in *The Angel in the House:*

> And in our love we dimly scan
> The love which is between Himself.

Doubtless there is a contrast between this mysticism and a harassed widower living in North London, struggling not only with material cares but with his own passions. Others besides Conrad have adopted an ironic attitude towards Patmore's celestial language and his very human wilfulness and weakness. Irony is rarely out of place in the tension which always exists between a man's character and his religion. But it would be a pity if such ironic smiles led critics to overlook the fact that such tensions are natural to religion and even to morality. Once a man living in this world tries also to live in the other, he has to some extent to make a fool of himself, as there is always comedy in that discrepancy and in that incongruity, and to this almost universal human folly Patmore was no exception.

If to some he seems more foolish than most men, that is only because he exposed his heart in his poetry and so laid himself open to ironic smiles. Very English in many traits, he was unlike the Wellingtonian Englishman of the nineteenth century and the old public schools in his lack of reticence. Yet there are passages in his verse on which no man would dare to be ironical, for they are so profoundly human that to smile at them a man would be in danger of smiling at himself. "The Toys" is one such passage. Another is "The Azalea":

> There, where the sun shines first
> Against our room,
> She train'd the gold Azalea, whose perfume
> She, Spring-like, from her breathing grace dispersed.
> Last night the delicate crests of saffron bloom,
> For this their dainty likeness watch'd and nurst,
> Were just at point to burst.
> At dawn I dream'd, O God, that she was dead,
> And groan'd aloud upon my wretched bed,
> And waked, ah, God, and did not waken her,
> But lay, with eyes still closed,
> Perfectly bless'd in the delicious sphere
> By which I knew so well that she was near,
> My heart to speechless thankfulness composed.
> Till 'gan to stir
> A dizzy somewhat in my troubled head—
> It *was* the azalea's breath, and she *was* dead!
> The warm night had the lingering buds disclosed,
> And I had fall'n asleep with to my breast
> A chance-found letter press'd
> In which she said,
> "So, till to-morrow eve, my Own, adieu!
> Parting's well-paid with soon again to meet,
> Soon in your arms to feel so small and sweet,
> Sweet to myself that am so sweet to you!"

There is a very real horror in that double awakening, for it exactly catches the agonizing tearing open of a healed grief which so often occurs at the moment of waking.

These moments of grief and painful tensions between past and present were exhausting Patmore's vitality. In February, 1864, and at the age of forty-one, he obtained leave of absence from the Museum, yielded to his friend Aubrey de Vere's suggestion, and set out for Rome, the city against which his mother's family and his wife had so often warned him.

VI

Travel to Rome

With a man of Patmore's poetic intensity, the background
was always an important element in the picture. Because he
believed more firmly than most men that the spirit was
constantly present in the flesh, for good no less than for evil,
every change in relationship or attitude or neighbourhood
affected him deeply. He was particularly sensitive to the
spirit of place. Paris and Edinburgh, Hastings and North
London, all had caused reactions or sympathies in his nature,
and he was to be even more influenced by country life in
Sussex.

It was natural that Rome, not the least impressive of cities,
should also have its effect on him, but it was hardly to be
foreseen that this should lead to his conversion to the
Catholic Church. There are indeed striking precedents in
the other direction, for Rome had a very different effect upon
Martin Luther. True conversion is seldom achieved by external beauty, however resplendent, for it occurs inside, in
the depths of the spirit. Men of the Reformation tradition
are more often repelled by a southern magnificence in religion. Nor are there many indications that this impressed
Patmore, who was as inwardly austere as he was sometimes
flamboyant on the surface. When he later came to build a
church himself, his ambition was to erect "the only Catholic
church in England which had no trace of bad taste." Some
might well have replied that certain of the Jesuit churches
already built, that at Bury St. Edmund's for instance, had

fulfilled this requirement, but that was obviously not Pat-more's view. He had little sympathy for the Jesuit and baroque styles; it is more probable that these were exactly what he meant by "bad taste." This is curious, when one considers how strong was the baroque element in his own character, but his artistic opinions were here more in line with the Pre-Raphaelites and their mediaeval sympathies.

Rome, for all its antiquity, is largly a baroque city, and had therefore little to commend it to him. Nor had he ever been attracted by travel, or by the Continent. It is difficult to see what led him to make the journey, which was a great strain on his constitution, weakened not only by grief and overwork, but by a persistent lung trouble from which he was rarely quite free. It is true that he required a holiday, but there were excellent resorts in his own country, whose charms he never underestimated, especially his beloved Hast-ings, to which he was so attached that he later settled down there.

His motive in travelling to Rome, then, cannot be traced directly to a quest for either health or artistic pleasure, nor was he the man to fall in easily with the suggestion of a friend such as Aubrey de Vere, who had made no secret of his hope for Patmore's conversion, unless he had already gone a long way in that direction himself.

It is clear, both from his own fragment of autobiography and his wife's sorrowful remark that the Romanists would have him after her departure, that he had already made this progress. His preference had long been for Catholic works in his religious reading, particularly for St. Thomas Aquinas. So it follows that in going to Rome he had also envisaged the possibility of going over to Rome, and it was in accord with the directness of his nature that in doing this he should in fact travel to the city itself.

In later years he realised that he had always been Catholic

in heart and thought. Indeed this was as clear in his case as it was to be with Chesterton. There was development after the act of submission but there was no violent break. His conversion was quite opposed to the spiritual experience for which the same term is used at revivalist meetings. He did not suddenly "see the light," but was slowly led to his decision by a long series of meditations.

He remained very much himself in crossing the Channel, in Paris belittling the Louvre and then cursing French food with arrogant insularity: "I find great difficulty," he wrote, "in getting anything to eat, except at the Tables d'Hote, which are long after my usual feeding time. At the hour I require a pound of steak and a pint of ale I go into the most likely-looking shop, and after walking three times round a table on which are thirty or forty different plates, I select what looks the most substantial, and bite a brown bladder of air; and end by making my luncheon off three ounces of perfumed sugar and one of chocolate. Unless they manage these things better in Rome, I shall die, or come back before my time."

On the Riviera he was hardly more satisfied: "The landlady gave me a bottle of very queer but quite drinkable wine, three eggs with the chill off (but without a spoon), and a bottle of oil. I drank the eggs and the wine, and might have drunk the oil, and had to pay only a franc."

This mellowed him, so that he was able to write, "The people here seem very harmless and good-natured, but stunted and ugly. They have good voices and a wonderful feeling for music. Such is the power of this lovely climate on the voice, that the cocks, instead of crowing as they do in England, bray loud and long like donkeys, and just finish off with a loose and rollicking imitation of a crow, by which alone I knew that they were cocks."

Once on the road to Italy he was enchanted: "There

appeared below me a series of scenes which, with all my uncommon sloth and indifference in the matter of sight-seeing, I could not but own to be, by themselves, well worth a thousand mile journey. For below, wherever there happened to rise a particularly insurmountable crag, there a little, lovely, faint-peach-coloured town crowded itself together, like a flock of sheep when the dog barks round it; and amidst it rose a light campanile, and the enormous ruin of some historic fortress, round which the town had originally gathered itself; the background, the brilliant Mediterranean, on which long lines of shining mist were still sleeping; the bounds, the sides of mountains so beautifully chasmed, chiselled, and dotted lower down with olives and oranges, that every square yard of surface had its interest; and the whole bathed in a spacious gulf of delicate air, burthened at intervals with drifting coils of golden and swiftly dissolving clouds."

The sensitive accuracy of this description proved that, in spite of his hankering after steak and ale, he had become a convert to the South.

Writing from Genoa, he was sufficiently restored to note details of the women's petticoats: "This greater elaboration of that part of the dress which is not supposed to be seen, unless by accident, is, I think, in high taste. At least, it is justified by the example of moths and butterflies, who commonly wear their finest patterns and colours on the under wings."

March 1864 found him in Rome, not very much impressed by St. Peter's: "There is a general feeling of space and convenience, very much like that of a great metropolitan railway hall."

He was more favourably inclined to the clergy: "I remarked the other night to a lady that, though I could understand the manifest pleasure with which the Sacred College and the rest chatted with the women, the preference the women showed for them was unaccountable to me. She assured me the women's pleasure consisted wholly in the thought of the penances their partners would have to enter upon next day. I do not however believe this: the real reason no doubt is that the Cardinals and Priests are by very much the pleasantest, best-informed, and most conversable people in Rome. The manners of one or two of the Cardinals, with whom I have had the pleasure of talking, are the most perfect I have met with. I have seen equal—never superior—refinement in other men, but seldom in combination with it so kindly a simplicity.

"Of all the characteristics of what I will call Roman Catholic manners the most attractive to me is the essentially un-English absence of reserve in speaking of subjects of the dearest and highest interest, combined with the equally un-English absence of cant."

But this did not lessen his amusement at the behaviour of a young German Catholic in a restaurant who had "crossed himself and had closed his eyes for some time with a ludicrous expression of acid ecstasy," and on opening them found that the waiter in error had placed before him Patmore's meat soup instead of his own abstinence fare: "He raised his hands in the air, crossed himself again, and commanded the waiter to remove the pollution from his sight, in a way which I am afraid made me smile in spite of myself. But when a lady passed near us and he looked at her with exactly the same expression and crossed himself again, and, after a few minutes, twisted his chair right round to have another look at her and again crossed himself with eyes closed in disgust and acid ecstasy, I had to turn away and blow my nose vociferously."

Despite this comedy, Rome attracted him. "I think far more highly of the administration here," he wrote, "than it is the fashion to think in England, and incomparably higher of the ordinary tone of ecclesiastical life, and of the effect of 'priestcraft' on the common people, who, as far as I can see, owe all the abundant good they have to the priests, and all their evil to the infection of the Revolution." He also referred to "the General of the Jesuits—a charming person, full of apostolic simplicity and innocence of the world."

For what revealed the essence of Rome to him was not the architecture but the people. He had interesting discussions with the Jesuit Father Cardella, who was to receive him into the Church. But his time was chiefly spent among the English Catholic colony in Rome, to which Aubrey de Vere had introduced him, and this had an important effect upon his future development.

There were three chief strains in the Catholic Church in England at that time to attract or repel converts: there were the Irish, the Continentals, and the old Catholic families with their dependents. They exhibited three different temperaments. With the largest group, the Irish, Patmore had little sympathy, either on political or religious grounds. The fact that they were the largest, especially among the clergy, was hardly likely to commend them either to his minority views or to his anti-clerical outlook. In politics too he was a violent Imperialist and apt to equate Ireland with rebellion. In religion the swiftness of Irish clerics at that time to damn the heretic jarred on his own sympathies, which led him to hail, as Catholic, ideas he approved, wherever he found them. The purity of Irish morals gave them an advantage with him over the French, but in essentials he had little more sympathy with the Continentals, perhaps less. There remained the older English Catholic group that he encountered in Rome.

From the first acquaintance, both his qualities and his prejudices drew him into closer sympathy with this group. Its members were intensely English, which commended them to him at once—English in an older and more traditional manner than their compatriots, for in their isolation they had retained the habits and outlook of an England that had vanished. That many of their families were pre-Reformation in origin was also to him a more authentic way of being a Pre-Raphaelite. Further, they had feudal and personal ties with the land, not in the style of the great Whig landlords who dominated England, for the Penal laws had much diminished their estates, but they maintained a more familiar relation with their farmers, some of whom shared their faith. Later, Patmore was teased by his friends to say exactly what he meant by the phrase "the mild and almost mythic time of England's prime," which occurs in one of his poems. It was, they suggested, a myth of his own. But it was probably something of this sort that he had in mind.

He was also openly impressed by the lineage of the old Catholic families, for he held that hereditary honour and example were some guarantee of character in a family. To what extent he was a snob is less easy to decide, for "snob" is a term for those who set the social repute above the worth of those they admire. When the English aristocracy was still respectable, it was not snobbish to respect it. Patmore was both too independent and too strongly attached to his own standards to respect social eminence alone, nor was he ever attracted by the fashionable as such, except perhaps in the matter of women's dress. Yet his association with the old Catholic families and something of exaggerated reverence in the tone with which he spoke of "great ladies" brought the charge of snobbery upon him. He rebutted the charge with indignant sarcasm and pointed out that "in my declining years I have scarcely a Countess on whom I can rely for a dinner." Accused of "entertaining 'flunkey' notions, not only of this life, but of the next," he replied, "I confess frankly to a general preference for persons of 'distinction,' and even to believing that they are likely to have a better time of it hereafter than the undistinguished. . . ." But he denied that he associated distinction with "wealth, culture, and modern Conservative politics."

It is this matter of "distinction" which best explains his attitude. Essentially a nonconformist, aristocratic in temper and welcoming idiosyncrasies, he was more at home with those who like himself stood out against the uniformity of Victorian England. His choice had more a personal than a class basis, in which he showed himself more Latin than English. He had other Latin tendencies which perhaps arose from this formative Roman period. His attitude to the clergy was always more Italian than English or Irish, in that he sometimes seemed to treat the Church more as a sister than a mother.

Certainly he was more at home in Rome than he had ever been in Paris. This was partly due to a vein of simplicity in the English and Italian characters, as against the more complex French, but the society to which Aubrey de Vere introduced him was also more congenial. The Roman intertwining of religion and culture corresponded to a fusion in his own nature; it was a climate very different from that of North London, where culture had largely developed, under the influence of Emerson, as a substitute for religion. It was also a climate in which he could grow more freely and more naturally, for art and religion came together in him as simply as in a Roman church, however uninspired he was by the baroque manifestations of them.

Rome enlarged his views, while the warmer air brought relief to his lung trouble. His health improved and in that more genial atmosphere he became less provincial. While he never achieved the cosmopolitan standpoint of such men as Conrad or Cunninghame Graham, with whose princely aloofness he otherwise had much in common, he did come to share

D

the less restricted outlook of that later generation, so that in the years before his death he was able to converse easily with less Victorian minds, such as Edmund Gosse and Alice Meynell—and even with Frank Harris, who was no sort of a Victorian.

Imperialist though he was, he never adopted towards the Continent the superior and missionary attitude of a Ruskin, nor did the fact that he was a Museum official lead him to admire works of art more than the spirit which had produced them. What he saw in Rome was the essential, the capital of a civilisation in which Britain had once been a province.

Yet inevitably, in view of his character, Rome itself could only produce its maximum effect on him when it was incorporated in the figure of a woman.

Among the Catholic circles in which he moved were two ladies, one of whom was so shy and withdrawn in character that she seemed clearly to be the travelling companion of the other, that poor relation or dependent who so often went with a single lady on a tour in Europe. Patmore was strongly attracted to her, even catching in her a resemblance to his dead wife, though in character she was very different, having little of Emily Patmore's determination, nor any of her gift for entertaining intellectuals and artists. She was entirely passive and feminine. To Patmore, already hesitating on the steps of the Church, she appeared the perfect embodiment of "Catholic sanctity." His wife had been bitterly opposed to Rome and had voiced her antipathy with some resolution. It is even possible that, with all her perfections, she had exercised more control over him than he had ever acknowledged, though all his life he constantly reminded himself of his debt to her.

To encounter a woman who was evidently unlikely to exercise any sort of control over a man, except to insist that he should be a member of her Church, at once opened all the doors for him, both those of the house from which his angel had departed, and the greater doors of the Church.

Yet he proposed to her before making his submission, only to learn that she had taken a vow not to marry, having also envisaged becoming a nun. He bowed and accepted the decision as final, not knowing that such private vows may be dispensed without difficulty.

But the issue which both he and she regarded as more momentous was still undecided. His thoughts and his beliefs had become wholly Catholic, but he was still reluctant to take the final step. The prejudices of generations, so strong that conversion at that period had almost the air of treachery to England, an argument to which he was peculiarly sensitive, the horror with which his mother's relations at Edinburgh had spoken of Popery at the very outset of his religious life, and the opposition of his dead wife, all these things kept him outside the Church.

Then suddenly he realised that these accumulated antipathies were not arguments but shadows which could only be dispersed by a decisive act of the will. Immediately he hurried to the Jesuit Father Cardella, insisted on being admitted though the house was already closed for the night, and demanded that he should be received into the Church there and then. Father Cardella refused this demand, but a few days later received him into the Church.

There was nothing sensational in his conversion, which was indeed belated. The desire had long been there. The change was simply brought about by the gradual overcoming of past emotions. It is also likely that the woman who resembled his dead wife helped him to conquer his reluctance to go against a wish to which death had given added force.

After his conversion he learnt that her vow not to marry was not an insuperable obstacle, and he approached her again, conscious that their shared faith had now brought them closer together. This time he was accepted.

But his joy was short-lived, for he soon learnt that this demure travelling companion was in reality an heiress, Marianne Byles, the daughter of a large landowner in Gloucestershire, herself a convert who had been received into the Church by Manning, following his own conversion. It was simply her self-effacing character which had led Patmore to make a very natural mistake. In reality it was the other lady, the more active and forthcoming person, who was the travelling companion.

Patmore was in great distress and even withdrew from the scene, feeling that he was in a false position and naturally reluctant to surrender his independence to a woman's fortune. But their many common friends intervened and the matter was the more readily smoothed over because he was even less the man to abandon a woman than to forsake his own standpoint.

Mary Byles—she was generally known as Mary—sensibly advised him to precede her to London and prepare his children to accept a new mother. From the beginning she had resolved to devote herself to them, and she reached happier and easier terms with these children of his than she achieved with adults, most of whom found her so shy and silent as to be difficult to approach. The most successful with her was the aged Barry Cornwall, nearly in his second childhood, who addressed her as his "dear Patmoria" and could permit himself the light impertinences which aid in approaching those who are too shy to encourage the more respectful.

There was little that Patmore could do in preparing his children, for the selfless Emily Patmore had already done what she could with the four older ones and was entirely successful with the girls, but the two elder boys, Milnes and Tennyson, were never reconciled to the second marriage; while the last two were young enough to pass naturally into the hands of their new mother. It is clear from the letters written at school by the youngest, Henry, that he was specially attached to her, and she indulged him with a particular fondness.

Emily Patmore had doubtless foreseen that her children would require a mother no less than Patmore himself would require a wife. As for natural jealousy, she had truly observed that she had filled a place in his life which no other woman could. He was no less convinced of that, and so, more remarkably, was the modest and self-effacing Mary Byles. She fully realised, she said, that she could never be what Emily Patmore had been, but she hoped at least to be a most loving mother to his children.

Patmore faced the change, which necessarily had some awkwardness in it, with characteristic frankness, even allowing himself a lightness which, while hardly delicate, was one way of overcoming the strain inherent in the situation. He remained implacably attached to his "Angel in the House," the Honoria who personified Emily Patmore, and he explained his attitude to Mary Byles herself by a play on Lovelace's lines:

> I could not love thee, Dear, so much,
> Loved I not Honor more.

It was a droll comment, which some have found grotesque, but it very accurately conveyed the distinction in Patmore's mind, and he was never a man to let a joke stand between himself and the truth. Indeed he rather cherished that form of wit, as a seventeenth-century poet might have done. According to Frank Harris, not the most reliable of authorities, but here not going beyond the known facts, Patmore once repeated to him these Lovelace lines (which are also to be found in a letter written to his second wife) in commenting on his second marriage. Harris said that he found it difficult to contain his amusement and "roared and roared" with laughter when he had retired to his room.

More strangely, Harris put this down to an absence of humour in Patmore and related it to a line in the poem "Amelia":

For dear to maidens are their rivals dead.

The irony in this line was surely intended by Patmore, but his humour was always of the "dead pan" variety, which sometimes takes in even men as worldly as Frank Harris, perhaps them more than most, for they are always readier to laugh at a man than with him.

Mary Byles at least seems to have been perfectly reconciled to the situation and to Patmore's treatment of it. Nor would the opposite method, that of belittling the merits of a first wife, be reassuring to a second, who could only wonder what her husband would say of her when she had gone, as Mary Byles might have come to fear in such a case, for she too died before him.

They were married at St. Mary of the Angels, Bayswater, by Dr. Manning, who had preceded Mary Byles into the Church and had felt some regret at her lost vocation. Before Manning's conversion there had even been some question of his marrying her. This fact and the correspondence that had earlier passed between Manning and her did not prejudice Patmore in his favour. He always spoke harshly of Manning, citing him as a type of the worldly prelate. Indeed, he suffered from a similar jealousy to that which afflicted the husband of Cornelia Connelly with regard to Wiseman, after she had founded the Society of the Holy Child Jesus, which Patmore's own daughter, Emily Honoria, was later to join. The circumstances in both cases were very exceptional, but they increased Patmore's constitutional antipathy towards the clergy.

After their marriage the Patmores went to live in High-gate, and for a year he continued to work in the British Museum. But this had always been a bread-and-butter job for the "young poet with the frayed cuffs," and his real work had been done in the evenings. Now he was a rich man, for these were days before the passing of Married Women's Property Acts, which explains his scruples about marrying a woman of wealth. His lungs, never robust, were a further reason for his retiring from the Museum. Later, to express his gratitude, he presented the Museum with a very rare edition of the works of St. Thomas Aquinas. Harris notes that gratitude was one of the dominating traits in Patmore's character. It was not only that, but also a basic element in his religion. His constant insistence on the joy of life and his bitter attacks on all those who railed against the order of the universe did not spring from his constitution or circumstances, which were upset more often than most men's, but from a lively emotion of gratitude to the Creator and to the Redeemer of life.

It was this gratitude which enabled him to surmount the griefs of his existence. There is little doubt that he suffered for many years, perhaps until his own death, from the loss of his first wife, for some of the most poignant expressions of his grief were in fact written during his second marriage, but his natural gratitude robbed the sorrow of bitterness. He followed Job in offering thanks for what he had been given and what had been taken away.

With the gratitude of Job, he also had the instincts of a patriarch. Rome was the origin of his second marriage, and the society he had kept there influenced his next choice of a home, for he had resolved to become a landed proprietor, to lead the patriarchal and feudal life which had so vividly appealed to his imagination. He chose an estate of some four hundred acres near Uckfield in Sussex. This included old farm buildings, but he built himself a respectable house which he called Heron's Ghyll. It was designed in Gothic style, but without the usual Victorian fantasies. Patmore's austerity and sound grasp of architecture insisted on simplicity, though stained-glass windows representing heroines of poetry added a flamboyant touch.

His conversion and marriage had taken place in 1864 and it was not until 1868 that the family at last moved into Heron's Ghyll, but much of the intervening time was passed in planning and designing with energy and enthusiasm. He was also much taken up with his children, writing to them and looking after their pets when they were at school. In the course of 1866 he wrote to his eldest daughter Emily, "I shall certainly be in town in a few days, and then I will come and see you, and bring you some apples and nuts out of the orchard. The squirrels are always scampering about the filbert trees, but there are plenty for them and us. Langley told me yesterday 'they wanted shooting.' But I told him they wanted no such thing, and that they were to live, even though they ate all the nuts."

In the following year he was giving news of a pet lamb: "Lamby is still alive. He dwells, literally, in clover, and is getting exceeding fat, and so boisterous and strong, that I am quite unable to hold him.

"Henry and Bertha each caught a fish in the pond yesterday. Mama and I had *one* of them for supper and it was quite enough."

Then the lamb became a ram and left them: "You will be both glad and sorry to hear that poor Lamby is at last gone to the place where all good lambs go. His life was never happy, for he never cared for company of his own kind, and was always hankering after human society—a sad example of how bad a thing it is for people to mix with those above their own rank."

There was also sensible advice at morbid moments: "You are quite mistaken in thinking you are born to be a trouble to everybody. You were never any trouble to me, but only a pleasure; and you will not be a trouble to yourself as soon as you get out of your present little bad habit of thinking about yourself. If you *could* 'understand yourself' I should be very much surprised, as it is very much more than much older and wiser people than you have ever been able to do. Other people, circumstances, and the grace of God will do that for you."

Patmore rejoiced that his wife Mary was so happy with the children, and it was a great pleasure to him when they moved into their new home. In managing the estate he showed a remarkable shrewdness, and took pride in it. He was delighted when a phrenologist declared that he would have made a successful man of affairs, and many observed that he looked more like a man of action than a poet. Certainly he was successful with Heron's Ghyll, for when he came to sell it later to the Duke of Norfolk, he realised a profit of nine thousand pounds. He even published a pamphlet on how he managed his estate.

Yet, as a poet, he took all this very much in his stride. Now that he could actually play the part of his Felix, hero of *The Angel in the House,* he was no less himself. Some critics have suggested that in Sussex he disguised himself as a squire, but it would be truer to say that he materialised, for he had always been that in spirit. He also resented the suggestion that a poet could not be a practical man, for he held that the deepest inspiration often enlarged the practical gifts, citing as an example St. Teresa of Avila, who told her daughters in Christ that "God walks among the pots and pans." Patmore's expression of the same truth was that "the presence of God includes presence of mind."

D*

VII

Second Spring

When in 1868 Coventry Patmore settled down at Heron's Ghyll to lead a new existence as a landed proprietor in Sussex, he was only forty-five, but he was already well into the second half of his life. He had written his most considerable work, *The Angel in the House,* which the literary world was content to accept as his masterpiece and a classic of the period, passing on to enjoy the excitements of Swinburne, the more readily because *The Angel* was now selling in its thousands and acquiring the sort of popularity that inclines critics to lose interest, both in a book and in its author. Patmore had his reputation. He was popular and no longer fashionable. It was time for him to retire and rest on his poetic laurels; and when it was known with what zeal he was cultivating his estate, people assumed that he had retired.

Yet if he had died then, his character would have small interest for posterity, while *The Angel* might have been forgotten or mistaken for society verse less lively than Praed's. Hardly a line of his prose or those brief sentences which contain his most characteristic thought would even have been written. Little regret would have been expressed for a career cut short, because it appeared complete enough—and in fact one of his three lives had indeed ended with the death of Emily Patmore.

In that same year in which Heron's Ghyll was finished,

the new Patmore appeared in print and was ignored, for in 1868 he sent his friends copies of nine odes which later formed part of *The Unknown Eros;* but few had any comment to make.

He was so disappointed by this reception that a couple of years later he burnt all the copies he could find of this small, privately printed edition. All his life he was given to burning; he also burnt copies of *The Angel in the House* at one moment when he suspected that some lines were out of accord with his beliefs, though it was that poem which had led Catholic friends to see in him a probable convert. But it was burning in any form that he enjoyed; he had the masculine passion for bonfires. As Heron's Ghyll was not a great way from Lewes, famed for its bonfires, strongly anti-Papist ever since the days of Mary Tudor, the neighbourhood was interested to know how the new Catholic squire would react to the bonfires of Guy Fawkes Day. Patmore's response was not only to have the largest and most splendid bonfire in the district, but to distribute cakes and whisky to all those who gathered around it. This gesture, characteristic enough to those who saw into his double passion for his country's tradition and his Church's gaiety, was greeted with astonishment. The fire threw a new light on Guy Fawkes. "What, burn him?" said one old man. "Why, I thought they worshipped him."

Patmore could not resist a bonfire, or a fire of any sort. Visitors to his home came away with a picture of him standing in front of the fire, his hands behind his back thrusting aside his coat-tails, or turning to heap more logs on the fire, smiling at his wife's gentle comment on his extravagance. Indeed, his richer life seems to have given him most pleasure chiefly in providing him with more logs to burn. Later, when he burnt, perhaps too hastily, his prose work, *Sponsa Dei,* he was probably as much moved by the prospect of a sudden

blaze as by doubts of its wisdom, for such swift and irrevocable gestures appealed deeply to him. But the burning
of the odes was not irrevocable, as his daughter Emily had
saved and secreted a few copies, and before long he was
writing more.

This writing and burning illustrates two currents in his
life at Heron's Ghyll. At one moment he was expressing
grief and anguish in the odes, for these first ones were the
most sombre, while at another he was standing in front of
a blaze, after an invigorating day on the estate, happy with
his family around him. Something of this country happiness
also appears in one or two of the earlier odes, but they fall
more naturally into the two parts in which they were later
published, the first mostly an expression of human grief, the
second a more mystical ascent into divine serenity. The
whole book, *The Unknown Eros,* did not appear until 1877,
three years after Patmore had left Heron's Ghyll for Hastings,
but they reveal his development over an even longer period,
dating from Emily Patmore's death in 1862.

There is ample testimony to Patmore's happiness in Sussex. Some have even said that he was like a schoolboy in
the enthusiasm with which he threw himself into managing
his estate, supervising the harvest, as he related in one of the
happier odes, walking with his dogs, or driving out with
his family and visitors—although on these occasions he sometimes became lost in reverie, with the result that he was
once or twice seriously lost on unknown tracks.

But most of the earlier odes bear witness to a very different current beneath this smoother surface. Sometimes in
a whole ode, as in the tragic "Departure," but more often
in chance phrases scattered through all these verses, he constantly showed his preoccupation with his dead wife.

The story revealed in this first part of *The Unknown Eros*
not only throws a very strong light on Patmore's character,

but largely contradicts the impression that he had consoled himself by making a happy and fortunate second marriage. One of these odes bears the significant title "Eurydice," proving that he too, another singer in the line of Orpheus, had descended into the underworld to search for his dead mistress. The images used very accurately suggest the misery of a man loaded with grief walking through a desolate city at night:

Thro' sordid streets and lanes
And houses brown and bare
And many a haggard stair
Ochrous with ancient stains,
And infamous doors, opening on hapless rooms. . . .

Other odes attempt consolation, and he says in "Winter": "It is not death, but plenitude of peace," finding in it:

The substance of things hoped for, in the Spring,
And evidence of Summer not yet seen.

But there is little consolation in the most revealing of these odes, "Tired Memory":

In agony, I cried:
"My Lord, if Thy strange will be this,
That I should crucify my heart,
Because my love has also been my pride,
I do submit, if I saw how, to bliss
Wherein She has no part."
And I was heard,
And taken at my own remorseless word.
O, my most Dear,
Was't treason, as I fear?

These lines state exactly what had happened. It was in no light mood of distraction that he turned to another love, but in a grievous acceptance of the necessity to live. The ode even relates how in Rome he caught a resemblance to his dead wife, "a strange grace of thee in a fair stranger." And this "fair stranger" was also touched by the tale of grief:

> And pure of faith, I think, to thee; yet such
> That the pale reflex of an alien love,
> So vaguely, sadly shown
> Did her heart touch
> Above
> All that, till then, had woo'd her for its own.

The poem concludes with the saddest line of all:

> But (treason was't?) for thee and also her.

This remorse must have been the undercurrent of his second marriage, perhaps of his whole life, for if, as has been suggested, his public, which appreciated *The Angel in the House*, would have preferred him to haunt his dead wife's grave, he himself was not untempted by that morbid devotion. But he broke away from it.

Was it treason? Patmore was the least suicidal of men, both by religion and by temperament, and such devotion to death could have been, for a man of his nature, a form of suicide. Psychologists claim that suicide usually springs from a motive of revenge, either on an individual or on life itself, but gratitude was too strong in him to allow him to be vindictive. Religion itself had assumed the form of his second wife, who brought about his conversion. He was hard pressed, not only by that but by the resemblance between the two women, the dead and the living:

> By thy delusive likeness doubly drawn,
> And Nature's long suspended breath of flame

Persuading soft, and whispering Duty's name,
Awhile to smile and speak
With this thy Sister sweet, and therefore mine;
Thy Sister sweet,
Who bade the wheels to stir
Of sensitive delight in the poor brain,
Dead of devotion and tired memory,
So that I lived again. . . .

These lines occur towards the end of the ode, "Tired Memory," and it is after this that he concludes with the question of whether it was treason—to both women.

For Mary Patmore, the self-effacing, was also involved in the remorse. She had accepted the secondary role, which would have been hers in any circumstances, as that was her temperament. Yet Patmore told her that he could not have loved her more, if he had never loved another woman before. This was probably true, for loving had increased his capacity for loving, which Miss Gore had woken in him as a boy and Emily Patmore in him as a man.

How far he had been unjust to Mary Patmore's destiny is a larger question, for if she had not married him she would probably have gone into a convent, certainly not into a more brilliant marriage or a greater position in the world. But there is some evidence to suggest that she might have been happier as a nun, and some justification for Manning's regret at her lost vocation.

She appeared happy enough at Heron's Ghyll, and later at Hastings, but her health, never strong, deteriorated and she was soon leading the life of a semi-invalid. She had lived in Sussex before her marriage—it was there that she had been a parishioner of Manning's—but she was not a woman for country pursuits, nor could she share in Patmore's enthusiastic rounds of the estate, nor was she quite at ease with

his great St. Bernard dogs. She was loved by the four younger
children, but the cares of the household and the entertain-
ment of visitors must have been a strain both on her health
and her shyness. Nor could she understand his poetic development in the later odes. True to her resemblance to Emily
Patmore, she was more at home with *The Angel in the
House.*

Her health might have suffered under the austerity of
convent life, but her withdrawn temperament, and possibly
a deeper vocational need, might have found there a satisfaction to outbalance that. Her one literary work, a trans-
lation of St. Bernard's *On the Love of God,* could have been
achieved even more happily in a convent. Beyond such
indications it is impossible to pry into what might have been,
yet in view of worldly speculations on the happiness that
women miss on retiring into a convent, it is perhaps worth
while to glance at the happiness that certain women sacrifice
by withdrawing into marriage. Possibly Mary Patmore was
one of these.

Yet there was a private chapel at Heron's Ghyll and daily
Mass. Mary Patmore dedicated herself to religion even in the
world, and some of her letters reveal both the breadth of her
generosity and the depth of her spiritual life. To a friend
in grief who did not share her religion she wrote: "My whole
soul is with the faith that at that beautiful bedside whence
the soul you loved went away, it went to a tenderer love
than any mortal love can be—was judged by love, was found
full of love, was excused any and all defects for the love's
sake that would have made them all up, had it known, was
passed on with reassuring reviving love to a place in the
realm of love where it is safe, with the consciousness of
everlasting safety, after a sight of the Eternal Beauty looking
on her in love which makes the present time an eager prayer
to be made fit to comprehend the joy of which she had a

taste, an eager craving for the purification and enlightenment which shall enable her to enjoy as the perfected Blessed do."

Mary Patmore was tender-hearted and she devoted herself to her husband and his children—there were none of their own union—with more compassion because they had lost a wife and a mother. There is no cause to doubt the reality of Patmore's devotion to her, if for no other reason than that gratitude was strong in him, and that, as Disraeli remarked of his own marriage, is in itself one of the most compelling motives of love.

Patmore may then be acquitted of treason to her, but the world was more disposed to accuse him of treason to Emily Patmore, since it knew him chiefly as the author of that great tribute to her, *The Angel in the House*. His remarriage and his conversion, both so intimately joined, cut him off from many of his friends, not only by their loss of sympathy with his ideas, but also by removing him from London. Many of those friends too, especially among the Pre-Raphaelites, had been fervent admirers of Emily Patmore. Indeed Patmore's isolation from them is one more witness to the extent of her influence and her charm. She had once written a story about men with tails, which revealed their true feelings in amusing contrast to the hypocrisy on their lips. Death also brought about some such revelation of truth, for the letters which Patmore had received on his return from Rome hardly concealed regret at the change in his life. Ruskin openly expressed his regret at the loss of a valuable ally, for Patmore would be "ineffectual," now that he had "turned Roman Catholic." To some extent this was true, for the unpopularity of his religion played as great a part as his own withdrawal in the eclipse of these years, one which lasted until he was taken up by a new generation, of which Edmund Gosse was to be the most influential.

Patmore soon realised that his new odes would not find

acceptance. In the Proem to *The Unknown Eros* he had written:

> Therefore no 'plaint be mine
> Of listeners none.

And he had compared his own songs to:

> . . . chants as of a lonely thrush's throat
> At latest eve,
> That does in each calm note
> Both joy and grieve;
> Notes few and strong and fine,
> Gilt with sweet day's decline,
> And sad with promise of a different sun.

Yet if these odes were not destined for a wide or an immediate public, they contained proof enough for those who were more intimately acquainted with his life that he had not loved lightly, that the flame of Emily Patmore still burnt within him. There is that moving ode, "Tristitia," in which he spoke of "Loss without measure, sadness without end," simply to assure her in the other world that if he failed to reach her heaven, she was not to let this cloud her happiness:

> Secure of my prime care, thy happy state,
> In the most unclean cell
> Of sordid Hell,
> And worried by the most ingenious hate,
> It never could be anything but well.

This is an unreasonable and, from one point of view, an absurd poem, but it breathes "the most ingenious" love. There are not many passages in English literature where such accents are to be found: in certain desperate abjections of love, human or divine, Patmore is almost alone, quite alone in his own age, while even in seventeenth-century verse this passionate intensity is rare. The ode is also interesting because, in contrast to the "Loss without measure, sadness without end," he also goes into some of those theological speculations which were to dominate his later life:

> For God is everywhere.
> Go down to deepest Hell, and He is there,
> And as a true but quite estranged Friend
> He works, 'gainst gnashing teeth of devilish ire,
> With love deep hidden lest it be blasphemed. . . .

In another ode, "If I were Dead," there is the desperation of a lover recalling a failure in love, with its strange conclusion:

> O God, have Thou *no* mercy upon me.

The greatness of such odes is that, while they perfectly express a desperate mood, they allow it to remain a mood and do not go on, as is so frequent in the poetry of despair, to erect upon a mood a false philosophy of life. What forces respect for Patmore is the absence of blasphemy in his private hell, because blasphemy is an attempt to blame what is outside personal responsibility. Patmore always remained responsible.

The same acceptance of destiny is finely echoed in "A Farewell":

> With all my will, but much against my heart,
> We two now part.
> My Very Dear,
> Our solace is, the sad road lies so clear.

These lines are the most accurate expression of his final feelings on the loss of the woman he loved, though they also universally speak for all lovers separated, whether by death or by duty. It may be useful to relate these odes to the circumstances in which they were written, for though this may not increase the impact of the lines themselves, it does awaken sympathy for the very human being who wrote them, and some have been kept from Patmore by antipathy for his character.

One difficulty in understanding such characters, however simple in themselves, is clearly brought out in another of the odes, "Let Be":

> Ah, yes; we tell the good and evil trees
> By fruits: But how tell these?
> Who does not know
> That good and ill
> Are done in secret still,
> And that which shows is verily but show!

Misjudgment of character, Patmore argues, is general, because however much a man struggles to widen his vision he can only see through his own eyes and cannot escape his limitations; he may see his own failures, he may even admire those who succeed where he fails, but he is incapable of judging those who fight different battles, leading to other heavens and other hells:

> But not all height is holiness,
> Nor every sweetness good.

The argument is comparable to that used by Browning in "A Grammarian's Funeral," but the range is wider, for it is not a drama of learning; it embraces the whole of life.

It is enlarged to a defence of the man whose defeats are obvious to the world, his triumphs secret:

> Haply yon wretch, so famous for his falls,
> Got them beneath the Devil-defended walls
> Of some high Virtue he had vow'd to win;
> And that which you and I
> Call his besetting sin
> Is but the fume of his peculiar fire
> Of inmost contrary desire. . . .

The ode shows that hidden aims may give a quite contrary meaning to the facts which are known to all:

> He fiercer fighting, in his worst defeat
> Than I or you.

This argument gives a personal application to the long and honourable line of defeats which, from Thermopylae or Roncesvalles to Warsaw and Dunkirk, have been more glorious than victories.

Then in conclusion Patmore turns the whole argument round to point out that the worst vices, no less than the greatest virtues, are hidden out of sight:

> Let be, let be:
> Why should I clear myself, why answer thou for me?
> That shaft of slander shot
> Miss'd only the right blot.
> I see the shame
> They cannot see:
> 'Tis very just they blame
> The thing that's not.

The irony of this last phrase is very characteristic of

Patmore. He had the sort of cynicism which seems more bitter than it really is, the sort which is based on a just acceptance of the facts, with the kindly veil of hypocrisy removed. This also appears in the strong lines of "Magna est Veritas":

> When all its work is done, the lie shall rot;
> The truth is great, and shall prevail
> When none cares whether it prevail or not.

Any historian, looking back on the long list of errors which have deluded mankind and had their day, is forced to admit the essential truth in these lines, that the lies which have misled a generation or more are in the end rejected not from any passion for the truth, but from the general human lassitude and thirst for novelty, which extends even to error. But it is not a comfortable fact, nor one to encourage the defence of truth. Patmore was a specialist in such disruptive facts. He presented them with a hard shell, because he was profoundly convinced that all truth is hidden, and necessarily hidden, as in "mysteries" in the old religious sense of the word, as in the Scriptural parables.

So in these odes he told the truth to his own discomfort, veiled indeed, but clearer to a posterity freed from the particular Victorian reticence of his day. There is a clear confession, for instance, in "Victory in Defeat," where he hears the command, "Come back, poor Child; be all as 'twas before," and answers:

> No, no; I will not promise any more!
> Yet when I feel my hour is come to die,
> And so I am secured of continence,
> Then may I say, though haply then in vain,
> "My only, only Love, O take me back again!"

This is one of the last odes of the first half of *The Unknown Eros,* and the final one tells of the fisherman's obedience to the command to cast forth the net again, though labour through the night has been in vain, with the result that he drew up:

> Not the quick, shining harvest of the Sea,
> For food, my wish,
> But Thee!

This is a peculiarly apt ending to the first half, which has echoed the despair of human love, for the second half is concerned with the love of God.

The whole of this first half, which contains Patmore's finest verse, is a poignant lament for Emily Patmore and in her person for human love, alternating with despair and self-reproach for his lack of fidelity and a recognition that the death of his love is also his own death.

Yet he survived. One life had ended, but his second marriage began another. This too was a life, but it was no longer a human love as the first had been. The bond that joined him to Mary Patmore was not one of nature aspiring to grace, but one that arose directly from their common religion, to which she had been instrumental in converting him. It is difficult to resist the conclusion that Patmore was now, in a sense, married to a nun, while he, though hardly a monk, was something of a recluse. Both were devoted to their religion, and their marriage might be described as one of religious convenience.

That might have been well enough, but there are discrepancies if this is to be regarded as a happy ending. There is no doubt of Patmore's passionate religious sincerity, but there is hardly less doubt that the same passions as had led him to celebrate human love and the beauty of women were

still at work. Indeed, they seem to have persisted almost to
his death, as he foresaw in the lines quoted above: he could
only be "secured of continence" and able to say "my only,
only Love" at the moment "when I feel my hour is come
to die."

It is this discrepancy that has drawn down most criticism
upon him. Some have doubted his mystical flights, seeing
him still so attached to the earth; while others, most indulgent towards earthly joys, have been put off by the
mysticism with which he treated them. The same critics
who accepted the contradiction between very earthly appe-
tites and the desire for heaven in a Villon, or in a man of
hardly less obvious Bohemian life such as Baudelaire, were
shocked to find the same forces at work in the bourgeois
poet of *The Angel in the House.* Patmore was not sensational
enough in his passions to arouse the sympathy which goes
today to the heroes of a Mauriac or a Graham Greene, or
to poets such as Villon or Baudelaire, but he·suffered from
the same human weakness. Where he differed from them
was that, regarding the heavenly fruits of love no less than
the earthly roots, he transformed the weakness into strength.
He was the opposite of a puritan, and it is by puritans that
he has been most criticized.

Patmore's chief offence, from a puritan point of view, is
one of his own definitions of sin, given in *The Rod, the
Root, and the Flower:*

"To call Good Evil is the great sin—the sin of the Puritan
and the Philistine. To call Evil Good is comparatively
venial."

Creation to him was basically good and was to be accepted
as a whole. To condemn even the lowest part of it was worse
than a too charitable judgment of an offence. This is certainly an anti-puritan attitude, but it is hardly an immoral
one. Patmore was an austere moralist in the sense that he

constantly struggled to dominate his own passions, but he could not endure without human love. He therefore sought to sublimate this love and to identify it as far as possible with divine love. He fervently accepted the traditional command of fidelity to one woman until her death, but once she had left the world—and he survived his first wife by thirty-four years—he found it impossible to remain faithful to her. That was the extent of his offence, but to a man with his view of enduring love it was one for which he reproached himself bitterly.

To an age unremarkable for constancy in love, this may seem a great pother about a small matter. Yet it sometimes happens that those who are themselves lax are quick to condemn the lapses of those with higher standards, and they are right, for men must be judged by their own standards. Patmore did not offend against the Christian law of marriage, but he did offend against his own ideal of absolute constancy. Emily Patmore's death remained the tragedy of his life.

Yet posterity may be heartless enough to reconcile itself to that tragedy, as in greater matters it has reconciled itself to the Trojan war, for from this tragedy came Patmore's great analogies between divine and human love, first set out in the second half of the *The Unknown Eros* and later worked over with greater clarity in his prose writings.

Briefly stated, Patmore's belief was this: the lover is to the beloved as God is to the human soul. There was nothing new in this, and Patmore never claimed to be original— indeed he expressly stated that he was only repeating forgotten truths. This was the stuff of all the Christian mystics. But he did claim that the nineteenth century, with all its romantic notions of love, had neglected this truth and was looking for the solution of love everywhere but in the place where it was to be found. For if human love was a rehearsal of the divine, it could only prolong itself and survive by a

constant offering of itself to God. The disillusionment which
attends so much human love was a proof that it had mistaken its own nature. Men and women were expecting more
of each other than they could give; only the love of God
could answer the desire of their hearts. Men had made a
god of love, when what they really wanted was the love
of God.

Since Freud, human love has been less honoured than it
was in the nineteenth century, and disbelief in God has
come to include disbelief in love. But this would not have
surprised Patmore, for he held that with most men human
love was a necessary stage in advancing towards the love of
God. First the natural, then the supernatural. Grace perfects
nature. Conversely, once men turned from the love of God,
they would lose even human love, which was only the shadow
cast by the divine.

These were the Christian commonplaces which Patmore
sought to express in the second half of *The Unknown Eros*.
It was only to be expected that he should be less successful
than on the human level, if for no other reason than that
it is easier to walk across a plain than to climb a mountain.
But there was more to it than that, for these later odes are
less authentic, less convincing, than the earlier ones. Judged
by the highest standards—as poetry that aspires to these
heights must be judged—they lack the strong practical sense
shown by St. Teresa of Avila or the passionate clarity found
in St. John of the Cross. Perhaps it requires a saint to write
of such matters. Evidently it requires a depth of mystical
experience that Patmore had not then, if ever, attained.
Yet in his last prose writings there are sudden reticences
and an assurance which suggest a deeper perception than
is to be found in the odes, while as poetry the earlier, more
human ones are both more sustained and more moving.
It may even be that he was right when he later wrote that

"the highest and deepest thoughts do not 'voluntary move harmonious numbers,' but run rather to grotesque epigram and doggerel." Such audacities are the finest things in these odes, as when Psyche exclaims:

> "Shall I, the gnat which dances in thy ray,
> Dare to be reverent?"

The emphasis of that "dare" has a greater impact than the odes as a whole. Patmore was particularly fond of that phrase and even quoted it later in his prose, writing of the love of God. It is a memorable expression of the gaiety which is rooted in humility.

These odes are most successful in their simplicity and in their meditations on the Incarnation, regarded, as Patmore later wrote, "not as an historical event which occurred two thousand years ago, but as an event which is renewed in the body of every one who is in the way to the fulfilment of his original destiny."

In "Sponsa Dei"—also the title of the lost prose work written later—there is a reference to the yearnings of first love, then:

> What if this Lady be thy Soul, and He
> Who claims to enjoy her sacred beauty be,
> Not thou, but God . . . ?

The next ode begins: "The 'Infinite'. Word Horrible!" That is a theme very dear to Patmore, who constantly turned from the abstractions of metaphysics to the simplicity of the Incarnation, as in this ode:

> For, ah, who can express
> How full of bonds and simpleness
> Is God,

> How narrow is He,
> And how the wide, waste field of possibility
> Is only trod
> Straight to His homestead in the human heart . . .

Both in this ode and in the one following it, theology
is naturally blended with sensual imagery:

> Who woos his will
> To wedlock with His own, and does distil
> To that drop's span
> The atta of all rose-fields of all love!

So in the following ode, "To the Body," he calls this the
"Wall of Infinitude," then passes to this exquisite sensuality:

> And from the inmost heart
> Outwards unto the thin
> Silk curtains of the skin. . . .

This blending of soul and sense was his commentary on
the Incarnation. He was at pains to assure lovers even in
one of the most mystical odes that:

> The full noon of deific vision bright
> Abashes nor abates
> No spark minute of Nature's keen delight.

In "Auras of Delight," with its striking opening line,
"Beautiful habitations, auras of delight!", he returned to
one of his favourite themes of childhood's revelation, which
he valued even more than Wordsworth, to conclude:

I *did* respire the lonely auras sweet,
I *did* the blest abodes behold, and, at the mountains' feet,
Bathed in the holy stream by Hermon's thymy hill.

The next three long odes, the bulk of the remainder,
are concerned with the myth of Eros and Psyche, in which
Patmore saw one more figure of God's love for the soul.
These odes are the most remarkable of all in their audacity,
for they take episodes of human love, even the most brutal,
and turn them into analogies of the divine. The cruelty
of love is compared to the scourging practised by ascetics.
It was such things as this that shocked some of Patmore's
closest admirers:

Should'st thou me tell
Out of thy warm caress to go
And roll my body in the biting snow,
My very body's joy were but increased;
More pleasant 'tis to please thee than be pleased.
Thy love has conquer'd me; do with me as thou wilt,
And use me as a chattel that is thine!
Kiss, tread me under foot, cherish or beat,
Sheathe in my heart sharp pain up to the hilt,
Invent what else were most perversely sweet. . . .

In the following ode Psyche explains to the Pythoness,
the prophetess whom she is consulting:

He loves me dearly, but he shakes a whip
Of deathless scorpions at my slightest slip. . . .

The Pythoness assures her that this is the way of gods:

"How should great Jove himself do else than miss
To win the woman he forgets to kiss;
Or, won, to keep his favour in her eyes,
If he's too soft or sleepy to chastise!
By Eros, her twain claims are ne'er forgot;
Her wedlock's marr'd when either's missed:

Or when she's kiss'd, but beaten not,
Or duly beaten, but not kiss'd.
Ah, Child, the sweet
Content when we're both kiss'd and beat!
—But whence these wounds? What Demon thee enjoins
To scourge thy shoulders white
And tender loins!"

To which Psyche replies:

" 'Tis nothing, Mother, Happiness at play,
And speech of tenderness no speech can say!"

Criticism of such passages raises the whole question of imagery. Obviously the difficulty with physical images is that they mean different things to the senses of different people. Even so simple a phrase as "the sweetness of divine love" may to some have a disagreeable flavour of candy that is too sickly. Yet images are necessary to men whose spirits have a body united with them. But when they are faced with the imagery of love, the most highly individual of human experiences, there is likely to be greater disagreement. Patmore's supporters, among them his daughter who became a nun, were most impressed by the purity which enabled him to use the most physical images with no sensual effect.

But that is precisely the difficulty, the word "sensual" itself, which may mean no more than "appertaining to the senses," but which in English has a strong suggestion of physical indulgence. In the most literal style, everything sensual must have a sensual effect. It simply depends on the individual whether this is good or bad, distinctions which reside in the heart, not in the senses.

These are very elementary considerations, but they raise problems which are everlasting. It may be true to say that there are passages in the Scriptures more sensual than any in Patmore; it may also be true that these are shocking to some people. The doubt in the mind of Patmore's critics is whether he was really the man to employ such language, whether he was a mystic or simply a lover. The doubt may well be justified, for he was both. What cannot be doubted is his sincerity. But sincerity may be an exaggerated virtue; the world has been littered with sincere crimes. What raises an ironical smile in some critics is the union in Patmore of sensual passion and religious fervour, both sincere. He may be reproached for not being a saint, or he may be reproached for being a man. But not all of his critics may feel in a position to make either reproach.

Perhaps the aptest comment on these Eros and Psyche odes is that implied in the line already quoted:

"Shall I, the gnat which dances in thy ray,
Dare to be reverent?"

For that is a conclusion in line with St. Augustine's "Love God, and do what you will," and the liberty of Patmore's language can only be judged by the intensity of his love, of which there is no measure.

The longest and finest of the concluding odes is "The Child's Purchase," probably written after Patmore's first visit to Lourdes in 1877, also the year in which *The Unknown Eros* was published. It is known that immediately on his return he sat down to revise and complete the whole series, written over the past dozen years, working with great rapidity, and this ode is an invocation of "the Lady of my Lord." It is a variation on a litany, with such phrases as "Hem of God's robes, which all who touch are heal'd," but it also returns to the joy of the Incarnation as against the abstractions of the Infinite. The Blessed Virgin is described

as "our only Saviour from an abstract Christ." That was
Patmore's most characteristic utterance, his protest against
the nineteenth-century watering of religion into philosophy
and God into "a power not ourselves making for righteousness." The same point is emphasized again here:

> Basking in unborn laughter of thy lips,
> Ere the world was, with absolute delight
> His Infinite reposed in thy Finite. . . .

The same ode contains a reference to St. Joseph's "rapture
of refusal":

> Mildness, whom God obeys, obeying thyself
> Him in thy joyful Saint, nigh lost to sight
> In the great gulf
> Of his own glory and thy neighbour light;
> With whom thou wast as else with husband none
> For perfect fruit of inmost amity;
> Who felt for thee
> Such rapture of refusal that no kiss
> Ever seal'd wedlock so conjoint with bliss;
> And whose good singular eternally
> 'Tis now, with nameless peace and vehemence,
> To enjoy thy married smile,
> That mystery of innocence;
> *Ora pro me!*

Patmore may have been led to this by words of St. Augustine which he quotes himself in *Magna Moralia:* "Joseph
was not less the father because he knew not the Mother
of our Lord; as though concupiscence and not conjugal
affection constitutes the marriage-bond. . . . What others
desire to fulfil in the flesh, he, in a more excellent way,
fulfilled in the spirit. . . ."

Patmore's comment on this clarifies his view of marriage—possibly his own second marriage had developed this—and explains how easily he could liken divine to human love:

> Every true Lover has perceived, at least in a few moments of his life, that the fullest fruition of love is without the loss of virginity. Lover and Mistress become sensibly one flesh in the instant that they confess to one another a full and mutual complacency of intellect, will, affection, and sense, with the promise of inviolable faith. *That* is the moment of fruition, and all that follows is, as St. Thomas Aquinas says, "an accidental perfection of marriage"; for such consent breeds indefinite and abiding increase of life between the lovers; which life is none the less real and substantial because it does not manifest itself in a separated entity.

The last short ode, "Dead Language," is an answer to those who accused him of writing too openly of the mysteries of religion, more decently treated in Latin:

> Alas, and is not mine a language dead?

This, the very last line of *The Unknown Eros,* shows that Patmore expected the odes to fall on deaf ears. He was right, for they were largely neglected until they were taken up a few years later by Edmund Gosse. Since that time, the earlier odes have received wide appreciation, and one or two have become standard anthology pieces, suffering in that less than much verse, for while *The Angel in the House* was easy to parody, the odes have a hermetic quality which protects them from imitation or ridicule. Even "The Toys," the most popular, remains moving, however often encountered, and some may well feel that the simplicity of the

E

conclusion expresses a religious emotion as deep as anything in the more mystical odes.

Evidently Patmore himself, who in later years was a good critic of his own work, felt that he could treat mystical love better in prose, for the subject of these later odes was also that of the lost *Sponsa Dei, The Rod, the Root, and the Flower,* and longer essays in *Religio Poetae,* which contain the fullest and clearest expression of his views.

He also came to believe that religious art is most effective when it is most human, not when it seeks to invade spheres which are too spiritual for imagery. In one letter he even declared that all religious art was a mistake:

> Last night I went by myself to hear Bach's "Passion Music" at the Albert Hall. As I like all Bach's secular music, as far as I know it, I thought it was a good chance of trying if I could get over my inveterate indifference to "sacred music," in common with all other "sacred" art. But my feeling that all religious art is a mistake was further confirmed. Indeed, a moment's reflection shows it to be so *necessarily* a mistake that one ought not to require experimental corroboration. Can the most expressive of all arts—poetry—attain to express the sweetness, sadness, or grace of life in any common human passion of love, pity, etc.? Nay, can it express the pathos of affection even in the voice and gestures of an animal? Carlo's, for instance, the other day, when I went to Heron's Ghyll and passed his kennel without unfastening his chain. What insanity then to write poetry and music about the Crucifixion!

He went on to criticize those who felt that a musical score

was "religious" because it was "slow," the same fallacy as that of the "dim religious light," which confuses the obscure with the sublime. "In art, as in life," wrote Patmore, "it is the most fatal of mistakes to think that we can get above ourselves. What we want is to become our true selves; and art can help us immensely by casting *light* upon the ground upon which we stand. . . ."

In the earlier odes he was his "true self," while in the later ones the "self" he was striving to become had not yet fully developed. "If you wish to influence the world for good, leave it, forget it, and think of nothing but your own interests," he wrote on the first page of *The Rod, the Root, and the Flower*. It was in this isolation that he was later to find himself.

VIII

Lourdes and Virginity

The grief that Patmore felt on the loss of Emily Patmore, and his more general meditations on marriage and its relation to divine love, had created *The Unknown Eros,* but they had also given quite a different turn to his thought. The more limited happiness of his second marriage and domestic life at Heron's Ghyll, together with the isolation caused both by his conversion and his withdrawal into the country, had thrown him back on himself. He was a more lonely man, and when marriage no longer filled his life as before, he was also forced to recognise its limitations as a philosophy of life. He began to realise that there were people in the world leading full and useful lives in which marriage played no part. Yet, so fundamental was marriage and the analogy between divine and human love to his whole outlook, he rebelled against this implication.

It was a problem that he had faced before, but earlier he had been content to claim for the married the virtues of the unmarried state. It is of interest that in the first draft of *The Angel in the House* he wrote that "wedded lives" were "fountains of virginity," and all his life he was anxious to affirm that the married had virtues on a level with the virginal. But later this more often took the form of asserting that virginity was a sort of sublimated marriage, an integrated personality with both its halves joined, or recalling the Platonic myth of difference of three sexes in one entity; and the last page of his last book, published in the year before his death, concludes with these words on virginity: "He who bears the flag is most the soldier, though he does not fight. And he who nobly upholds the honour for which man is procreated helps as much as any the conservation of the race."

Yet his thought had constantly revolved the other way. One of his most impressive aphorisms asserts that "Mother is more than and includes Bride." It is an idea which illuminates, but it might have been even more true to say that "Bride is more than and includes Mother," in the sense that it is virginity that includes all the potentialities of life, as the child includes the man. This was the argument of Hopkins in his most profound poem, "The Leaden Echo and the Golden Echo," where men are urged to give beauty back to its Begetter where it will be kept, "with far fonder a care kept."

This is one of the most practical arguments in favour of virginity, that it is an untapped source of energy necessary to men and women who dedicate themselves to the most selfless and sacrificial tasks. But that was not Patmore's way. He was the poet of marriage, and he was not one of those poets who can write spiritedly remote from their inspiration; he was also a man who so constantly thought in terms of the masculine and the feminine—in literature and in art, no less than in the individual character—that it would almost have split his personality to remain single.

Some who have most sympathy for Patmore's religious views have been puzzled by the contrast between his three marriages and his intense devotion to the Mother of God, one of whose primary aspects is virginity. This clearly represented some mystery and conflict in his own nature, as for many years after his conversion, which took place in 1864, he had reproached himself for being "hopelessly out of

harmony" with the feelings and practices of Catholics towards the Blessed Virgin. This is already odd enough to
anybody familiar with Patmore's mind who would have
assumed that it was precisely this which was the source of
attraction, even some years before his conversion, when he
was first drawn towards Rome. Yet at that time he apparently had no such feelings, for in one of the odes he wrote
of those years:

> When clear my Songs of Lady's graces rang,
> And little guess'd I 'twas of thee I sang.

Evidently for many years he had remained ignorant of
this. Yet from the date of his conversion in 1864 the subject
worried him—for thirteen years, in fact. The way he chose
to conquer his aversion was to make a pilgrimage to Lourdes
in the year 1877. It was there, he says, in his autobiographical
fragment, that he rose from prayer "without any emotion
or enthusiasm or unusual sense of devotion, but with a
tranquil sense that the prayers of thirty-five years had been
granted." It was from that moment that his intense devotion
to the Mother of God dated.

Thirty-five years—it is a remarkable period. That went
back to the time when he was nineteen, when he was first
seriously thinking of religion at all, for his father had brought
him up without any religious instruction; and in the course
of those thirty-five years up to the time when, at the age
of fifty-four, he knelt at Lourdes, he had written *The Angel
in the House,* which friends had considered Catholic in
spirit, he had become a Catholic himself, known for the
force and fervour of his convictions; and during all that
time he had remained out of sympathy, not only with one
of the central aspects of his new religion, but with what most
people would have seen as the dominating inspiration of
his entire life, even from youth.

It is not only a mystery but a contradiction. How could he, whose ideal was the Eternal Feminine, have found himself in opposition to its chief expression in religion, when that religion was also his own?

The explanation sheds a strong light on Patmore's character, for it is clear that it was the very force of his devotion to woman and marriage which made the idea of virginity repugnant to him. It was for this reason that he claimed, in the passage of *The Angel in the House* later suppressed, that the married were "fountains of virginity"; he could not bear the idea that there was any virtue in virginity which was beyond the reach of married virtue, despite the fact that most virtues involve some limitation of those which are, not indeed opposed to them, but more consonant with a different sort of personality.

In this failure to see any merit in virginity, he was characteristic of the nineteenth-century English, at once so high-flown in their conception of love and so prolific that the failure to reproduce seemed also a lack of patriotism. "Increase and multiply" was not only a religious precept, but a social commandment to people the great red spaces on the map of Empire. Even Chesterton, who in writing of the Victorians recalled that he was born a Victorian himself, cited virginity in his *Orthodoxy* as a thing in which he saw no merit himself, but was content to take on trust as a flower of which he had not been told "the beautiful or terrible name."

But Patmore lacked Chesterton's humility: if he could not feel in body and soul a fierce partisanship for an idea, he was often enough bitterly opposed to it. Perhaps too respect for virginity comes more naturally today, as in the later days of the Roman Empire, when the disorders of instinct have given to innocence the charm of green fields against the squalour and confusion of an urban wasteland.

But this was a thing which Patmore only with difficulty grasped. It is an important point, for it is the main criticism to be directed against his entire philosophy. Virginity has a priority over marriage, for men are born virgins; they only become married. Further, every sort of heroic endeavour and many forms of suffering and disease enforce this lonely virtue. Most religions, and few more than classical paganism, have accorded a special respect to virginity.

It is doubtless true that virginity and marriage depend on each other; it would even seem that those ages which have accorded most respect to virginity have also been those which most honoured marriage, and conversely, as today, lack of respect for virginity also loosens the marriage tie. Yet in the Victorian age there was certainly respect for marriage; virginity was represented by those maiden aunts without whom family life has required aid from the state. But the decline had already begun, and the thwarted virginity which lacks any inspiration outside itself and is only a form of selfishness aroused a distrust against the whole idea.

Yet neither this nor his championship of marriage is quite enough to explain Patmore's antipathy, for he became increasingly aware of the interdependence of marriage and virginity. That he himself felt a lack of balance in his outlook is proved by his determination to go to Lourdes; for he declared that he went precisely because the place had become the centre of a devotion to the Virgin Mother of God for which he had no great sympathy. It was unlike him thus to bow to anything which had not yet fully taken possession of his heart and mind. It was much more like him to utter his sympathies and antipathies with the utmost candour; he was quite unchecked by any human respect, least of all when it was clerical. Nor did he usually so much submit to the Church as enter into a marriage with her in which he was a somewhat dictatorial husband, so that it occasionally seemed almost as though the Church had been converted to him rather than he to the Church.

Yet on this particular point he was submissive and discovered a humility which was by no means frequent in his often arrogant and always independent character. There is something very moving in the spectacle of this man of fifty-four, a famous poet and a thinker headstrong in his opinions, going to a country which he always disliked and kneeling in a township that had achieved fame only through an apparition to which he had never been attracted. He has recorded that he received there the change of outlook which his will, but not his mind nor his feelings, had demanded, and that this changed outlook remained with him for the rest of his life.

It is possible that in some respects what happened to him at Lourdes was more important than what had happened at Rome, his original conversion in 1864, for then he had long been Catholic in sympathy, but this was the gift of a sympathy which he had not felt before. That he realised the greatness of the change is proved by words he wrote later: "The Pagan who simply believed in the myth of Jupiter, Alcmena and Hercules [in which the god assumed the form of the absent lover Amphitryon] . . . knew more of living Christian doctrine than any 'Christian' who refuses to call Mary the 'Mother of God.' "

This has the vehemence which a man sometimes uses when referring to opinions that he has renounced. It is true that Patmore had not made that particular refusal—he had been antagonised only by more special devotions to the Mother of God. But such references, which occur chiefly in his prose, for he had almost ceased to write verse after the rapid but brief period of work which resulted in the revision and publication of *The Unknown Eros* in 1877, soon after his return from Lourdes, indicate that he had come to feel

*E**

as strongly in his sympathy as he had previously felt in his antipathy.

It is not difficult to uncover the reason for both, for it is clear that he was so obsessed with the idea of marriage, and in particular with the idea of first love as a decisive revelation of divine truth, that he had difficulty in conceiving religion otherwise than as the love between God and the beloved soul. Where most religion ends, in the final raptures of the mystics, his began. Even in the first part of *The Angel in the House* he had written of first love:

> That, and the Child's unheeded dream
> Is all the light of all their day.

What is interesting in this is that the Child's dream went so long unheeded by Patmore himself. He realised, or he would never have written these words, that innocence is the greatest of revelations, but he failed to note—or rather his excessive preoccupation with marriage blinded him— that innocence is also virginity.

Nothing could better illustrate the dangers of mysticism. Patmore began with mystical love; it was the basis of his religion. But mysticism demands innocence, what he called "the Child's dream," which can only be recaptured by a long process of purification. He had been acquainted with suffering and death, but in his exaltation at the discovery of divine love—it was so like him—rushed madly forward without passing through the intermediate stages, one of the violent who take heaven by storm. It was at Lourdes that he recovered what he had missed.

Yet he wrote in his *Aurea Dicta* that it was never possible to recover in heaven what had been sought against order. "You may, by great repentance, get something better, but never that." It is possible to doubt whether he ever quite incorporated this new knowledge into his philosophy, which was too restricted by the bonds of marriage. When he made the remark quoted above that "Mother is more than and includes Bride," he was still praising marriage at the expense of virginity. Such praise is always acceptable to mankind, a larger portion of which is married than unmarried, but there are certain difficulties in Patmore's philosophy of marriage at which he sometimes briefly glanced only to dismiss them in a truculent and Johnsonian style, but sometimes with less than Johnson's earthy common-sense, as when he said that "marriage is open almost equally to all, except, perhaps, the less wealthy members of the upper orders." These difficulties largely spring from his refusal to admit that the person is ultimately more important than the marriage, and that the pre-eminence of virginity is an insistence on this truth.

This resentment against virginity, which is common enough in the world—the popular saying, "I'm no plaster saint" is often a manner of expressing it—is natural and easily understood as the resentment of a majority against a minority exercising a virtue which to many people does not appear a virtue at all. It is often behind criticisms of monks and nuns made even in Catholic societies. To some extent it is healthy enough; there is not always much to be gained by admiring a condition of life which is quite outside a man's own destiny. Men are not obliged to admire doctors or soldiers, even if they are often so unfortunate as to have to consult or to rely on them. The matter only becomes serious when men claim their own way of life as the only one and dispute the right of others to lead theirs. Patmore was far from this type of bigotry, though his anti-clericalism was no doubt partly due to his prejudice against celibacy. Yet his favourite daughter became a nun and remained closest to him and the most valued and most intelligent critic of his life. He constanly struggled to admit the virtues of virginity, and there are passages in *The Rod, the Root, and the Flower* which show the stress of this compulsion, some of them very finely, for a man often writes his best when his admiration is grudging. But the point sometimes appears laboured, as it had to be, for Patmore was really struggling to make good a flaw in the foundations of his philosophy.

Marriage is one of the most difficult things on which to base a philosophy of life, because it is beyond the scope of an individual. That is obvious enough: no man, no woman, can create an enduring marriage, for the simple reason that the husband or the wife may at any moment walk out of the house and never return. Of course the peril is doubtless one of the attractions, and marriage survives despite it; but the risk, like the risk of death, is one on which many people prefer not to dwell. The opposite view, of marriage as a paradise, a life "happy ever afterwards," occupies the foreground, rightly, as most people think more often that they are going to live than that they are going to die. It is also true, perhaps less fortunately, that the majority of happily married people are apt to blame those who fail in marriage, as prosperous business men blame those who lose money. But the mischance exists, as bankruptcy exists, as disease exists—and with illness there is even a healthy opinion that it could have been avoided if the sufferer had been more sensible.

Such healthy opinions are necessary to society, which rightly requires that the norm should be one of success and health. But when a man is constructing a philosophy to embrace the whole of human life, he has to take the disasters into account, for it is often in their treatment of evil that philosophers fail to give satisfaction.

Patmore was supremely healthy in mind, not always in body, which makes the health and vigour of his thought all the more admirable. In a characteristic essay, "Cheerfulness in Life and Art," he wrote that "life is not only joyful, it is joy itself" and affirmed that "the opportunities and hindrances of joyful life are pretty fairly distributed among all classes and persons." He was at his best writing in this vein, pouring scorn on romantic melancholy and declaring that it was a vulgar error to consider Dante a melancholy poet— "joy is nowhere expressed so often and with such piercing sweetness as in the Paradiso" and then, supreme Patmore touch, "The Inferno is pervaded by the vigorous joy of the poet at beholding thoroughly bad people getting their deserts." This last is all the more incongruous coming from a man who was constantly exercised by the problem of Hell and insisted that God's love reached to it. But he finishes by a point which seems to him to clinch the whole matter of the joy of life: "Marriage is open almost equally to all . . ."

This may be true; but some have doubted whether, in a world that has left the Garden of Eden behind it, marriage is always and universally a source of joy unalloyed. Patmore believed that marriage led people to God. What sort of marriage?

> Well wed is he who's truly man,
> If but the woman's womanly.

That closed the matter for him, and perhaps there was much truth in it at the time he wrote these words, though he was constantly lamenting the decline of manliness in England and particularly in literature, while he had a horror of feminism, until somewhat corrected in his views by Alice Meynell. It may be true that, as Johnson also maintained, any man and any woman may marry with much the same expectation of happiness; but Patmore wrote very precisely, and in a world where many men are not truly men, nor women womanly, his definition reveals its own inadequacy.

What then weakened the force of his arguments when he closely pressed the analogy between human and divine love, was precisely this fallibility of human love. The woman who is suffering from the infidelity, the cruelty or the simple inadequacy of her husband is unlikely to be moved by the consideration that her marriage is a symbol of the relationship between God and the soul, or may even despair of a heaven which so much resembles what to her has become a hell. Those who warned Patmore against pressing these analogies too far had something to be said for them, though the reasons they urged were often enough mistaken.

Their complaint was usually that the distance is too great, that it is irreverent to compare human with divine love. This objection moved him not at all, for he pointed out that the Sacrament of the Altar "affirms and acts a familiarity which is greater than any other that can be conceived," as God there descends into the flesh of the communicant.

He was also as a poet peculiarly alive to the use of symbols, and this made him equally impatient of those who considered certain symbols "wrong" or unsuitable to certain subjects. There were and are many, for instance, then and now, shocked by the mystical interpretation of the Song of Songs. It is, they argue, so very physical, so very sensual: it can only be the language of lovers. But Patmore at least understood such symbols, understood that the more truly and the more faithfully, the more physically even, such language was used, the more perfectly was it the *symbol* of divine union, than which nothing could be more intimate.

It was in this symbolic manner that he pressed many other analogies, disturbing those whose minds or temperaments were closed to the meanings of symbols—perhaps even to the meaning of poetry.

For, however short human experience falls of the ideal love, it remains the most useful analogy of the divine because it does contain the idea of reciprocity—often inadequately, for often one loves and the other only allows herself or himself to be loved, but reciprocity is constantly envisaged and regarded as a necessary condition of happiness. Those who refuse the analogy, insisting that God is too far above human affection to make it valid, not only substitute fear for love and diminish the fatherhood of God, but by a strange inversion take too much upon themselves and in their remoteness from God unconsciously assume the lonely pride of the atheist, whose serenity springs from the conviction that there is nothing in the universe superior to man.

Human love with its hope of reciprocity gives a different meaning to the love of God, a term loosely used and sometimes confined to the love that man feels for God, which may have no more than the hopeless exaltation of the lover towards what is beyond his reach, "the desire of the moth for the star," which is too often not only a folly but a disaster.

But the love of God in its specially Christian meaning is the love which God has for the world and for man who is his child. "God so loved the world." At times, as a Patmore and other mystics would put it, this love can even have the hopeless aspect of human love, for man has the freedom to put himself beyond the reach of God's love. This idea of reciprocity, even in the relations between Creator and creature, is so essential to Christian thought that the loss of it is much more dangerous than the perils of pressing too far the analogy between human and divine love.

It is also true that the language of religion has to be simple if it is to enter the hearts of ordinary men and women, to whom love, whether it is in the heights or the depths, is always love—there is no other word to describe it.

In spite of Patmore's aloof and aristocratic air, his conviction that "the world has always been the dunghill it is now" and that its only purpose was to nourish some rare "flower of individual humanity," he had, as is not uncommon with reactionary pessimists of his sort, a great sympathy with ordinary men and women, and this certainly affected his determination to present religion simply as the divine counterpart of human affection. Its simplicity, even its obviousness, had a special value for him. He even asserted that the religion revealed by God to mankind had to be obvious on the face of it; it would not be a proper revelation unless it could present its evidences freely and openly to every man, the most simple no less than the most intellectual, in an appeal to self-evidence in which, for Patmore, all reasoning ended. He even denied that there were two sides to a question; there was only one, "and this side only a fool can fail to see if he tries," though he corrected the aspersion this appears to cast on the obtuseness of those who fail to see the truth by constantly insisting that people were really Catholics at heart, for he was one of those who apply the term Catholic freely to anything they like or approve. The ease with which he identified the Church with his own favourite opinions was only equalled by the ease with which he ascribed Catholic thoughts and feelings to those he liked or admired.

He was a fervent egoist in all such matters: that was what assured his independence. The same egoism led him to see his own vision of human and divine love as possessing a far wider, almost universal, validity. Yet at the same time he declared that he would be horrified if "a charge of originality" was brought against him. He claimed that he was only repeating ancient truths, "digging again the wells that the Philistines had filled," as he never tired of quoting. Here again the traits of the patriarch are to be discerned; he is a commanding figure, yet a type of his family and the chosen people, uttering again the words which were spoken by the prophets.

IX

The Patriarch

Patmore's life in Sussex at Heron's Ghyll from 1868 to 1874 and later at Hastings from 1875 to 1891, before he passed to his final backwater in Lymington, where he lies buried, was one of meditation on the great love of his life, on the nature of love itself, and on its transformation into the divine. But there was also an outward life, such as all men have forced on them or invent for themselves, either to satisfy conventions they respect or to fulfil some secondary need of their natures.

Yet with Patmore this outward life was more closely related to his real inner life than with most men, for it was based on his children, the children of his dead wife. The two eldest, both boys, Milnes and Tennyson, were grown up, out in the world, and there was little contact with Milnes, except in such paternal acts as finding the money to buy him a ship of his own. But the other four were very much a part of the family, and of them the eldest, Emily Honoria—so called after her mother and her mother's inspiration, the Honoria of *The Angel*—and Henry, the youngest, were especially close to their father, not only in convictions and cast of mind, but also in love of poetry and appreciation of his.

Both moreover had an importance of their own. Henry had a small volume of verse published, and there are a few lines on him in the *Dictionary of National Biography*, though he died at the age of twenty-three, while Emily has more recently had her biography written by a member of the religious community she joined.

It was in the care of his lands, and with his children—particularly these two—around him, that Patmore's life began to assume a patriarchal character. There was always an ancient and oriental strain in him; his sympathy for the Turks was not only based on Gladstone's opposition to them, and hostile critics, regarding his three wives as if they were living simultaneously, have even written as if he kept a harem. That is excessive, for his marriages were within the Christian tradition, though in some ways he went back to a much older tradition, in a sense pre-Christian, for he was essentially a patriarch; and there have been patriachs who did not confine themselves to three wives.

Yet this was a bizarre element in his destiny—to have three married lives, each of approximately the same duration, fifteen years, each happy in its way, and each marked by a different style in his work. He suffered from this peculiar situation chiefly in the loss of his first wife, which was the cause of it. But once he realised that he had to survive her, he accepted it more lightly, as a necessity of his outward, rather than his inner life. He was highly amused when the only child he had by his third wife, learning that he had been married three times, exclaimed, "Why, Papa, you're half as bad as Henry VIII." He repeated the story with glee, a suitable joke for a patriarch.

But the tragedy, that of his first wife, was repeated in the two children who were closest to him and most like her, Emily and Henry, for they were also like her in dying prematurely, Emily at the age of twenty-nine and Henry at twenty-three.

Yet while they lived, his life as a patriarch at Heron's Ghyll and Hastings was still in them a prolongation of his first marriage. Emily, in particular, bearing her mother's name, gave him an even greater understanding, for she shared both his religion and its development in the odes, which had been feared by her mother. She had been a remarkable child. Even her childish remarks showed originality as well as humour. When her parents had wrapped her up and taken her out to witness the magnificence of a night sky, she turned her eyes to the stars and remarked, "How untidy the sky is." The first sight of the sea inspired her to a remark no less exact: "How soapy."

A third remark gives a similar but deeper insight into her mind: when being bumped up and down on the knee of an indulgent relation, she said, "Please don't, you'll shake out all the sawdust." From this it is clear that she was one of those who go direct to the inner essence, jumping over the outward fact. She hardly needed the image of a doll, going straight to the stuffing, the heart of the matter. She had the Platonism of childhood, but in her it survived childhood. She read ardently her father's verse and was one of his best critics. Indulgent, she compared the odes to Scripture, but more exactly defined the parallel by saying that they were simple enough for anybody to read, yet so profound that very few could really understand them. Her grasp of the essence in an image gave her this understanding. In one way it was greater than her father's for while he was content with the image of divine love in marriage, she went direct to the reality and became a nun.

She took her first vows in a convent at St. Leonard's in 1875—it was the year in which the family had moved to Hastings from Heron's Ghyll, after a brief period in London, where Patmore had insisted on her going to the opera and tasting social life before coming to a decision. The society she joined was that of the Holy Child Jesus, which had been founded on Wiseman's initiative by an American, Mother

Cornelia Connelly, whose strange story had an odd resemblance to Patmore's own preoccupation with marriage and the love of God. She had been the wife of an American clergyman who became a Papist, and she had followed her husband into the Church. They then travelled to Rome, where her husband aspired to the priesthood, which was only possible if she became a nun. She quickly responded to his devotion and took her vows. In Rome Wiseman, who was looking for a woman of ability to start a society of nuns devoted to education in England, formed a high opinion of her gifts, and his choice fell on her. She gave herself to this task with the utmost zeal and holiness. But the husband, who had become a priest, had a relapse and demanded her return. It is probable that jealousy of Wiseman's influence had an even stronger effect on him than jealousy of Manning's over his second wife had on Patmore. At last he reached the point of appearing in a yacht off the coast of Hastings and threatening to abduct Mother Cornelia Connelly. He also pursued her through the courts, where the case created an immense sensation: the British were almost startled out of their phlegm by the spectacle of a Popish priest pleading with the Archbishop of Canterbury's legal representative—at that time responsible in such cases—for the return of his wife, who was a Popish nun. The court decided for the husband, but Mother Cornelia's counsel at once gave notice of appeal. This appeal was successful.

The husband then devoted himself to making virulent attacks on the Church of Rome, and some of his pamphlets proved very popular. This was unpleasant for Mother Cornelia, but she also suffered in a more human way because he had control of their three children—there had been a fourth, but he had been killed as a child through being pushed by a dog into a vat of boiling sugar. These children were lost to their mother's Church, though one of them returned to it after her death. Their father finally settled down as minister to the American Church in Florence.

It is unfortunate that the story of the Connellys so closely resembles the plot of a very bad novel, for it was not trivial in its effects. It aroused strong feeling against the Roman Church in England and it produced the Society of the Holy Child Jesus. Mother Cornelia, steeled by the tragedies and sufferings which have attended the birth of so many religious orders, persevered and there were ten convents of her foundation in England and America at the time when Emily Patmore joined the one at St. Leonard's. She could hardly have chosen a society whose history was more in accord with her father's own religious and human tensions.

The sympathy between father and daughter persisted. A friend said of them, "It appeared as though they had one mind in two bodies."

Her death in 1882, seven years after taking her first vows, affected Patmore only less than the death of his first wife. Emily Patmore had died again.

She too, the eldest of the girls, had been a mother to the younger children and had accustomed them to the idea of his second marriage, while it was she who introduced Harriet Robson, her own friend and companion, into the household, where she was able to take over many domestic tasks from Mary Patmore, who was an invalid in the last years of her life. She died in 1880 and in the following year Patmore married Harriet Robson.

She was witty, intelligent, competent, but a closer contemporary estimate of her character is lacking, as she survived the period after his death when most was written about him. Strictures have since been passed on her which establish that she had no reluctance in becoming the wife of a famous man whose possessions were also greater than her own. But Patmore had also his own distinction as a lover, and the combination was one which might have attracted women who were not acquisitive. It is also certain that in the daily company of a charming and intelligent woman Patmore needed no encouragement, so it is possible that a too indulgent or mistaken view of his character might lead to a too harsh judgment of hers.

The attraction existed before Mary Patmore's death. Emily, in a letter written from her convent a year before her own death, admitted that she had expected this third marriage, and she welcomed it, not only for the sake of her two younger sisters and brother, Henry.

Henry, the youngest of the six children of the first wife, was almost as close to his father as Emily and had with him an ease which shows that to him at least Patmore was no domestic tyrant. Henry was gay and light-hearted in the home and outside it, as no son could be whose spirit was in the least crushed by his father. He always referred to his sisters as "hags," maintaining that, from the same Greek derivation as hagiography, this was a tribute to their saintliness. When one of them, in the reproving manner of elder sisters, reminded him of a saint's day, he gravely produced his tobacco and said, "I will smoke an extra pipe in his honour."

He was also on the happiest of terms with his stepmother, Mary Patmore, and was one of the few who penetrated her reserve to reach intimacy, for he had the light impertinence which breaks through the barriers of withdrawn natures. He teased her over her one foible of concealing her age, and as there is the same uncertainty over the age of fishes, began his letters from school to her with "Dear Old Fish," which again hardly suggests a typically Victorian attitude towards parents.

He was on similar terms with Patmore, who was as taken with his verses as his own father had been with his first poems. When Patmore praised them, Henry laughed and told his father that perhaps one day he would only be remembered as "the father of Patmore." In a preface written to his son's poems, Patmore quoted this remark and added that, if he had lived, this would probably have come true.

Yet Henry was not precocious. He was gay, even about his poetry, so often the grave spot in the gaiety of young men, and he had the lordly way of talking about it which only springs from genuine modesty, as when he said, "I might write like Longfellow or one of those second-rate poets. . . ." In the same vein he declared, "I don't know what sort of a poet my father is—but he is certainly an excellent critic." Questioned further, he explained, "He admires my verses."

His health was not good and once, during a retreat, the retreat-master thought he looked strained and told him to go into London and amuse himself. Consequently a lady acquainted with the family encountered him at Verrey's, eating ices—the same taste as his father had in a crisis of his young manhood. At once he warned her, "You must not speak to me, I am in retreat."

His verses were admired by critics as discerning as Edmund Gosse and Richard Garnett, who regarded them as a "psychical phenomenon" in their startling combination of real originality with paternal influence, a form of heredity for which there are more parallels, though few enough, in painting than in poetry.

Perhaps the most moving are the lines he wrote when already in view of his own early death:

The birds have something they must say
Before the light has gone away.

He died in 1883, a year after his sister Emily. He was twenty-three.

They were the last reflection of Patmore's first wife, and although he was to survive until 1896, it was in these years of final loss that friends remarked how he, who had preserved youthfulness and vitality beyond middle age, suddenly became old. A last child, by Harriet Patmore, was born in 1883, the year of Henry's death. Christened Francis Epiphanius, he was known in the family as Piffie. His father took a great delight in him, able to enjoy all the incidents and excitements of his childhood, as had not been possible in the laborious years in which his first six children had been born. But he was already sixty: already the gaunt features of the Sargent portrait were apparent in him. The charm and delicacy of youth had vanished, and this last son was the late child of a patriarch.

Yet, despite this rapid ageing, the patriarchal figure had not come into being quickly. The years of Heron's Ghyll and Hastings had all gone to its making, developing his very English character, and the roots of his prejudices were both softened and hardened by the soils in which they grew. Heron's Ghyll itself had been named after the birds which haunted it, and Patmore also had an aviary erected there. This concern with birds and animals was not a fresh trait in his nature, for even in Highgate days there had been a dormouse which lived in his inkstand and watched him at work. The children maintained that ink was its chief food.

But, though devoted to animals himself, he detested sentimentality towards them in others. Once when a lady came to the house and gushed about animals, expressing her horror of those who could be guilty of any cruelty to their pets, he got up and went to the door, where he paused.

"Where are you going, Mr. Patmore?" she enquired.

"When I hear anybody talking like that," he replied, "I always go out to the stableyard and give the dogs a thrashing all around."

This pleasing gesture would have had exactly the effect he desired, had not one of his daughters, with the tactful disloyalty of women to the foibles of their men, revealed the truth the moment he had left the room, "Papa does not really do it, you know."

He did not really do it, but this is not to say that he did not feel strongly in the matter. There are plenty of similar indications in his writings. He claimed that much humane feeling was "due to a softening of the brain rather than the heart," and that "huge moral ill" aroused less pain among humanitarians than "the yelp of a poodle which has had its ear pinched." In an essay on woman, in which he ascribed any discontent on her part to a failure in men, he declared that "a large proportion of our male population are thrilled with effeminate pain if an injury is done to the skin of a cat" but showed no indignation "at the violation of every sound principle."

Comments on such remarks are likely to spoil their effect no less than his daughter's discreet intervention, yet perhaps their point is only sharpened when it is remembered that the man who made them was devoted to his St. Bernard pups which were, naturally, the finest ever whelped. His daughter Bertha, who had a gift for drawing which won interest and encouragement from Ruskin, drew an excellent likeness of one St. Bernard—once again the daughter may serve to correct the father's opinions.

It was in a letter to Bertha that he wrote of this St. Bernard, " 'Bismarck' is now under the hands of two doctors, and is taking three kinds of medicine. His pills are most imposing." Here the letter showed a large blot, the size of the pill. "The sight of them is quite humiliating to humanity, which is only capable of"—and a very small blot, hardly larger than a full stop, showed the size of a human pill.

His was a masculine outlook, more sporting than sentimental. Basil Champneys, his future biographer, was astonished to hear the remark, when Patmore was watching him fishing, "I said seven 'Aves' for you to catch that fish."

His dislike of sentimentality towards animals was a part of his disgust with teetotalism, vegetarianism, and campaigns against smoking. He referred to wine and tobacco as "natural stimulants to good impulses and fruitful meditations." He only took to smoking in his later life, but then with great gusto, and Gosse noticed that cigarettes were scattered about his room "thick as autumnal leaves . . . in Vallombrosa." He once said that if it was completely proved that smoking shortened his life, he doubted whether he would give it up, as it stimulated thought, which was the essence of life. One of his last poems even suggests a tolerance towards smoking in women:

> With, 'twixt her shapely lips, a violet
> Perch'd as a proxy for a cigarette.

One of his injunctions to Harriet Patmore, when he was away from home almost for the last time, was, "Don't spare the port wine."

Gosse remarked how curious it was that so genial a man should have more often been regarded as the image of austerity, hardly less false than the earlier picture of him as a sentimentalist. It is perhaps the patriarch in Patmore which has led some critics to see him as a typical Victorian figure. But the Victorian patriarch had in him a mythical element which is absent from Patmore. Both Carlyle and Ruskin were substantially different from the patriarchs, not only in being childless: their beards were genuine enough, but the Biblical riches of their language were largely false, in that they were magnificent antiques surviving from a tradition which no longer commanded the intellect of the country—nor even their own. Both Carlyle and Ruskin were prophets in foreseeing the fate of a great commercial empire; but they were not Jobs blessing the Lord who gave and took away—they more closely resembled Roman senators of the early centuries lamenting the decay of virtue and a corruption which threatened the state, the public thing. Their concern was less with religion than with the social condition of their country; and in their different ways they developed ideas which are still to be detected in contemporary Socialist thought.

Patmore stood on the other side of the barricade, as his opinions were those of an instinctive, though intellectually coherent, diehard. His politics had the pessimism of Dr. Johnson and he even abhorred the new conservatism of Disraeli, who had passed the Reform Bill of 1867 and extended the vote to fresh classes of society—the act of a dangerous revolutionary. He resisted the whole current of nineteenth-century political thought; as a patriarch he could only lament the decline of personal government. He could agree with Carlyle that mankind were "mostly fools," but unlike Carlyle he did not seek a political remedy. For him the collapse of the existing social framework was only a part of the general collapse in manners and tradition. In certain moods he even saw beyond his own pessimism to the triumph of truth in another generation, "when none care whether it prevail or not."

More than most of his contemporaries he foresaw that the coming crisis would be one of conviction rather than political or social organization. In an essay, "Christianity and 'Progress,'" he enquired whether the Founder of Christianity proposed "that everybody should have plenty to eat and drink, comfortable houses, and not too much to do? If so, Communism must be allowed to have more to say for itself, on religious grounds, than most good Christians would like to admit."

Since his day Christians, not all of them tepid in their faith, have come to avoid such antitheses between material and spiritual growth, and have accepted the challenge of Communism. It is an inconsistency in Patmore that he, who laid such emphasis on the body and its necessary share in the spiritual life, should have refused to admit that society, which is only the body of mankind, could also receive the spirit. His God had come down into the human body, but not into the body politic.

There was more than one reason for his political attitude, though it was as often expressed by defiant prejudices as by any process of reasoning. First, he was conservative by temperament and by vocation as a poet, because he always looked backwards to the golden age of childhood, an attitude which easily leads to the asumption that all change is for the worse and to the further assumption that the historic past was also better than the present, especially as the art and poetry of the ancients, or even of Elizabethan England, was evidently superior to that produced by the Victorian age.

Yet here again he was inconsistent, for he said that we often mistake our childhood for the old time, which we would really have found "as intolerable as our own," and concluded that "the world has always been the dunghill it is now."

Then, as a Pre-Raphaelite sympathizer, he was drawn to the Middle Ages, and the same process of thought which turned William Morris into a Socialist led Patmore to conserve the shadowy remnants of the mediaeval English society which had survived into the Victorian era. In the older Catholic society he encountered in Rome he found more of that than he might have discovered if his acquaintance with the English aristocracy had been wider. In particular, his passion for architecture not unnaturally found more to stimulate it in the Middle Ages than in Victorian England.

Sometimes, in fact, he was so disgusted with the ideas of his own age that he condemned them as a whole, becoming in the most exact sense a reactionary. No doubt his own isolation contributed to this. If he had found more people to agree with him, he would have made those readjustments in views which are always necessary when private prejudices become public opinions. In other words, his politics were not quite serious. In one or two of the odes they are simply amusing, as in that on the Second Reform Bill of 1867 which he described as:

. . . the year of the great crime
When the false English Nobles and their Jew,
By God demented, slew
The Trust they stood twice pledged to keep from wrong. . . .

These were strong words for a measure which left property as the basis of the franchise, though it was true that it had not been expected from the Tories, who had passed it only to "dish" their opponents—that was the "great crime."

It is at least clear that Patmore was not an orthodox member of the Tory party, so to stigmatize one of its most successful manoeuvres. Gerard Manley Hopkins later took him to task over his reference to Disraeli, arguing that since Disraeli was a Christian, there was not even the excuse of an argument for this gross appeal to racial prejudice. But Disraeli himself brushed it aside with the remark, "I am in England and Patmore is in Patmos," which was not only witty but true, as Patmore certainly had much more of the Jewish visionary in him than Disraeli.

But Gladstone, as a greater villain, received a greater ode, "The Standards," when he wrote "an incendiary pamphlet" against the English Catholics which urged them to resist Papal Infallibility as their ancestors had defied the Armada.

He was waving "the black flag of Hate." There was also a reference to "the Powers of Hell." Yet Patmore protested, in the essay on Distinction which so shocked Alice Meynell, that he was "an unpretentious and sweet-tempered old gentleman," and to prove this point declared, "I am willing to believe that, were we admitted to the secret recesses of their souls, we might discover some apprehension of the living truth of things in Mr. Gladstone, some conscience in Lord Rosebery. . . ."

He was as broad-minded as that. These references at least show that, in the great Victorian debate on the relative merits of Disraeli and Gladstone, which had replaced earlier arguments on God and the Devil, he was as independent as in other matters.

He was in fact more critical of the politics of his age than of the political parties. "Democracy," he wrote, "is only a continually shifting aristocracy of money, impudence, animal energy, and cunning, in which the best grub gets the best of the carrion." But this was more a criticism of mankind than of democracy, since the acquisitive have prospered under any system of government. Yet he associated the decline in moral standards with the great Victorian optimism about the future of mankind, believing that this slackened the fibres of moral effort. So it was with horror that he envisaged a future in which the demand for material progress would lead to Government supervision of private life, and "we shall have to 'square' the district surveyor once or twice a year, lest imaginary drains become a greater terror than real typhoid," for an inspection which occurs at regular intervals can be more irksome than an isolated outbreak of fever. Then minor human indulgences might be more harshly judged than any sins, and civic virtue might lead to a new hypocrisy, that of the prig who was "in a continual state of deadly sin." Then too might arise a "despotism which will have to be mitigated by continual 'tips,' as the other kind has had to be by occasional assassination." This imaginary prospect so daunted him that he preferred human frailty to progress of this sort, which once led him to say, "It will be an unhappy day for England when the mechanic takes to becoming a sober, respectable man."

That day has since arrived and to the majority of men may seem less dreadful than the prospect he described, but it is true that other forebodings of his have been echoed by contemporary thinkers, even by some in general sympathy with Socialism. Some housing programmes, which condemn cottages for their lack of amenities not always desired by their occupants, show that "imaginary drains" may yet become "a greater terror than real typhoid." To some the district surveyor is more formidable than any member of the Government. Probably this was always true, in that the feudal baron was less feared than his agent on the spot, but Patmore at least foresaw a political change discerned by few of his generation.

He wrote little on politics, and little of what he wrote needs taking very seriously, for he was deliberately provocative and really based his criticism on the fact that reformers were too concerned with drains and diet, indifferent to the far deeper personal and moral forces on which society really depends. Yet it would be a mistake to dismiss his politics too lightly, as they sprang not only from his patriarchal attitude, but from an element in his religion. He followed those who, from St. Augustine to de Maistre, have emphasized the action of Providence in the world and met the attacks of those who blamed human disasters on the nature of the universe, rather than on the nature of mankind. More personally, he was disgusted by the complaints and writhings of those romantics who were disposed to blame anything but themselves for their misfortunes. He criticized "a wilful melancholy, and, the twin

sign of corruption, a levity which acutely fears and sym-
pathizes with pains which are literally only skin-deep. . . ."

Against this he constituted himself, as others of his religion, a defender of the established order of the universe.
But some have made the false deduction that they must also
defend the established order of this world—and its prince,
who was more traditionally identified with the source of
all evil. Patmore also laid himself open to this charge, making
it possible sometimes to associate him with those Catholic
Conservatives of the nineteenth century who were often more
anxious to stop the breaking up of large estates than to
encourage the spreading of their faith. No doubt there were
some genuinely unable to distinguish between the attack on
property and the attack on religion, but it was noticeable
that some defended their property with considerably more
fervour than they practised their religion.

It is natural that the poor should be more revolutionary
than the rich. This quarrel and this confusion, which went
far back into the Middle Ages, were accentuated by the
French Revolution, and brought about that identification of
clericalism with conservatism against which the Christian
Democratic parties are still struggling today. What is startling
about Patmore, once again showing how his independence
escaped from the ordinary categories, is that he was himself
bitterly opposed to clerical influence.

X

The Anti-Clerical

The roots of Patmore's anti-clericalism spread as widely as those which nourished his politics, though in different directions.

Osbert Burdett has suggested that the poet of marriage, who proclaimed that "the proper study of mankind was woman," so much preferred the company of women to men that this both affected his capacity for friendship with men and led to an antipathy for bachelors, especially priests. Yet he was friendly with men as different as Gosse and Carlyle, Ruskin and Frank Harris, Francis Thompson and Robert Bridges. He even numbered priests among his friends, Gerard Manley Hopkins and Monsignor Rouse. He also enjoyed the company of priests and cardinals in Rome. Yet it is evident that he preferred women to men and that among men he sometimes preferred listeners to talkers, though he was content to listen to Carlyle and to Hopkins.

He had a certain arrogance in later life, which Sir Herbert Read has attributed to lack of affection in his mother and lack of reliability in his father. If this is so, the compensation of arrogance was only taken when he no longer required it, though his isolation may have created a later need to reinforce his position. A man of similar assertive personality, Hilaire Belloc, who knew how to be scornful, once admitted, "I know that all contempt is acid, and that no man drinks it to his profit," and the contempt that Patmore had for many ideas of his age may also have led to self-assertion. What is relevant here is that a man of such temperament, with a keen interest in theology, was unlikely to be most at ease with priests, who were in a position to correct him on this subject.

A French critic, Agnès de la Gorce, has viewed him as a lay theologian, typically English in his desire to twist doctrines to suit his own convenience or temperament. This is to suggest that it was his Protestant background that made him anti-clerical, and such was the view taken by some of his contemporaries, who believed that he was too much of "a true Englishman" to accept a Catholic discipline. Another French critic, Valéry Larbaud, has taken exactly the opposite view. He believed that Patmore, in proclaiming his independence of the clergy, was anxious to show his fellow-countrymen the distinction between the man and the priest, to assert that religious truth was unaffected by the immorality of priests or Popes, historical instances of which were the commonplace of religious controversy at that date.

Certainly the point of Patmore's anti-clericalism will be missed, unless it is remembered that his loyalty was never in dispute and that the least hint from Hopkins, for instance, of anything weak in his theology was sufficient to make him correct it at once. He accepted the Infallibility decree, such a stumbling-block to some, with enthusiasm, even writing an ode in which he hailed it as "no uncertain blast" blown from "our Sion of the Seven Hills," the same ode in which he so vigorously attacked Gladstone, who had written against the decree. Yet he was careful to point out to his friends that other papal pronouncements were "the personal opinions of an amiable old gentleman," in no way binding upon himself.

This supports Larbaud's view that he wanted to show his fellow-countrymen that his religion was quite independent of the personal character and opinions of individual priests, as against that of the chapels and revivalist movements which often depended almost wholly for their effect on the ardent personality of a single minister. Surely Larbaud is also right in suggesting that the reason why Patmore went out of his way to ascribe a Catholic flavour to eighteenth-century writers who bordered on the erotic was that he wanted to disturb the excessive puritanism of his age. He genuinely hated the sort of narrowness and hypocrisy which had led to the bowdlerising of Shakespeare. In an essay, "Ancient and Modern Ideas of Purity," he lamented that "the fig-leaf has invaded the Vatican itself" and recalled the outspokenness of the Fathers of the Church, even citing "the words of Her, who is the model of innocence to all ages, in her answer, at thirteen years of age, to the message of Gabriel."

It was in the same spirit that he asserted that it was just as Catholic to have a statue of the Venus de Milo on the mantelpiece as one of the Blessed Virgin. This was characteristic of his desire to upset the conventional, especially those in his own communion, but it was also his way of claiming that all the highest pagan ideals were included in Catholic civilisation.

In these matters he intended to shock, and like all people with that intention—he was like Belloc again in that—he measured his words more to his audience than to his own thoughts. But he was anxious to shock Catholics no less than Protestants. What distressed him most was that he discerned a similar narrowness in those of his own faith. In the same essay on Purity he wrote, "Strange to say, this modern notion of purity is not limited to those churches which owe their origin to the Reformation." Then he contrasted the old idea of purity as "a sacred fire which consumes and turns into its own substance all that is adverse to it" with the more recent idea that it could only be preserved by being frozen. In his opinion "the foul puritanical leaven of the Reformation has infected the whole of Christianity," and in another passage he said that "the Catholic Church itself has been nearly killed by the infection of the puritanism of the Reformation."

On this issue he was even more critical of Catholics than of Protestants, for he felt that they were betraying their own heritage, and he was indignant that they accepted the narrow standards of the society in which they lived. He even referred to them as "the most ignorant of all people, modern Catholics."

He had his own view of the Reformation, as of so many other matters, for he maintained that no man went to the stake for a point of doctrine, but only for his essential faith, so that both Catholic and Protestant died for the same religion. There is more than his aloof perversity in this, for the Reformation was a civil war, only less in England than in France and the German lands, and it is true that in a civil war both sides die for their country.

The interest of some of Patmore's pronouncements—they are hardly arguments—on such themes as these is in the serenity with which they cut across the ordinary lines of controversy in a way disconcerting to both sides. There is a breadth in his judgments, yet this is never the sort of "broad-mindedness" which rests on indifference to the issues or a watering down of principles. The freshness of the approach arose from a genuine independence. He was never conventional in his thinking, nor did he feel obliged to champion certain events or arguments simply because he was a Catholic or simply because he was an Englishman. He was faithful both to his religion and to his country, but he was free from some national and religious prejudices—though he had plenty of his own—which had grown from history, not from the realities themselves. His historical sense was sometimes acute: Carlyle once startled him by saying that he was the only man who could write a history of the Anglo-Saxon peoples. He professed that he had not the least idea what Carlyle meant, but the union in him of a very Anglo-Saxon heart and freedom from Anglo-Saxon cant may have provoked the suggestion from Carlyle, who in *Past and Present* had shown his awareness of an earlier England which was more congenial to Patmore's mind.

Patmore's historical sense also allowed him to avoid that timidity in English Catholics developed in them during the years in which they had been despised or persecuted, and that excessive reliance on the clergy which more often springs from uncertainty of mind than from a genuine respect for the priesthood. Reaction against this was another source of his anti-clericalism.

There were also personal reasons. He had had an unfortunate series of chaplains at Heron's Ghyll. Most of them were aged invalids. One was in constant need of nursing. Some demanded his oldest wine or other comforts. It was natural enough that they were an indifferent selection, as priests were urgently needed all over the country, and only those who were quite unfitted for more important work could be assigned to a post so limited. But his anti-clericalism was chiefly inflamed by an event which occurred after his move to Hastings.

By 1874 the estate at Heron's Ghyll, which he had developed so successfully, proved too large for the family, and Patmore sold it at a very handsome profit to the Duke of Norfolk. In the following year he was offered the Mansion House in the old quarter of Hastings, exactly the house in which he had vowed to live when he was a boy. Hastings had other associations for him, and the alacrity with which he accepted this offer is another proof of his devotion to his first wife, Emily Patmore, for it was here that they had passed their honeymoon, and here that he had returned soon after her death, to recapture the past. Her daughter and namesake, Emily, was also able to go to the convent, close by at St. Leonard's, in which she became a nun. Hastings was in every way suitable, and it was at the Mansion, a much easier journey from London, that he later welcomed such friends as Gosse and Hopkins.

When Mary Patmore died in 1880, he formed the idea of building a church dedicated to St. Mary, Star of the Sea, as a memorial to her. To this end he entered into negotiations with the Pious Society of Missions, whose representatives wished to establish a centre in that neighbourhood. Basil Champneys, his future biographer, was the architect. Instructed by Patmore, who had very strong feelings on the fate of the project, he has included a record of this in his biography. Patmore even insisted that anything written about him should contain his own full account of the matter.

Plans were made and the building proceeded. Patmore's agreement with the Society was that he should provide the church itself at a cost of five thousand pounds, while the Society should provide the land, schools, priest's house, and the furnishings and crypt of the church at a cost of eight thousand pounds. To meet these expenses the Society was obliged to raise a mortgage. Patmore knew this, but he had understood that it was to be raised on their London property. He became extremely indignant when he found that they had raised the mortgage on his church, and he wrote a letter to *The Tablet* in which he laid the full facts before the public.

His indignation was doubtless exaggerated, for it was unlikely that the Pious Society of Missions would go bankrupt or that its creditors would take possession of his church, an eventuality which his strong protest envisaged. In fact, he behaved in this affair with all his father's indiscretion. But there were other forces at work: his personal feelings were involved, as the church was a memorial to his dead wife, whom he did not want associated with a mortgage. There was also his distrust of the clergy. Indeed, it is difficult to say whether this incident provoked his anti-clericalism, or whether his anti-clericalism provoked the incident. It is only certain that his feelings towards the clergy were not more amiable afterwards.

The church was opened in 1883 and still stands as a memorial, not only to Mary Patmore, but also to her husband's architectural good sense, for Champneys admitted that he was a most inspiring person to work for and had a high degree of technical understanding in their discussions, during which he was able to make valuable suggestions. He claimed that it would be the only Catholic church in England without any bad taste in it, but unfortunately, owing to his trouble with the Pious Society, it left a bad taste in his mouth.

Yet his testiness on the subject of the clergy dated back before this. It was also aroused by the sort of pious lady who gushed about her favourite priests and who could not understand how disasters could ever befall the faithful. One of them talked in this style about a Catholic church that had been burnt down. It upset her greatly, as if it was due to an oversight on the part of Providence and had been mistaken by the heavenly powers for a heathen temple. This idle sectarian chatter was abhorrent to Patmore, but he undertook to enlighten her and gravely explained that he knew exactly why the church had been burnt down.

She begged him to tell her.

He told her: "The priests burnt it down to get the insurance money."

There was a horrified silence, until she bravely rallied and tactfully changing the subject enquired whether he was not very sorry to hear that a certain priest was dead.

"No, I was very glad," he answered.

Such conversations are the more impressive when it is remembered that the man delivering judgment had so much the look of an Old Testament prophet that Sargent depicted him in this role. Patmore was far from serious on such occasions, but he was one of those men who put their whole personality into their sallies and are no less striking in their humours than in their solemnities. Yet he must have been excessively provoked by such pious chatter, for he was on most occasions courteous to women, both by temperament and by conviction.

It is possible that his anti-clericalism was often more provoked by remarks passed about the clergy, indicating what he considered too slavish an attitude to them, than by the clergy themselves. Indeed there is something a little ridiculous in any sort of anti-clericalism among believers, for the clergy are drawn from every walk of life and any criticism of them is only an attack on the general body of believers. But this wider attack was probably Patmore's intention, for he was impatient of a timidity among English Catholics, some of whom were still inclined to lie very low, as if there were still informers lurking around to imprison them and butcher their clergy. In the middle of the century there were still men and women living who could remember the Gordon riots, when not only property but lives had been in danger. This tendency to hold back was natural enough, especially in families which had made great and sometimes mortal sacrifices for their religion. But it was hardly conducive to fervour or boldness in public debate.

Patmore, in his quieter time, was himself very much at home in England, despite his fierce opposition to many of his fellow-countrymen's ideas and despite his complete devotion to the religion of a minority. Nor was he the man to adopt an apologetic attitude for his views. This led him to dislike any segregation of those who shared his religion, and he welcomed anything that brought them into closer touch with the life of the nation. He saw too that this was often achieved by an acquaintance with ordinary human failings, and he ironically commented, "It cannot but soften the most religious tradesman's heart to find that his brother-tradesman, who holds the Catholic faith, will, as a rule, cheat as readily as he will himself."

This remark is typical of his attitude towards those who shared his faith. He was the last man to claim for them merits which they did not show in daily practice. He had none of the sectarian, almost sporting zeal which leads some to claim for the side they support—like a football supporter—all the good qualities and to deny them to their opponents. He was rather more inclined to praise the other side, for he expected higher standards from his own and was proportionately disgusted when it failed to live up to them. In fact he sometimes treated members of his own Church as some men treat members of their own family, with that disconcerting affection which notes their failings with a certain relish.

It was the same with his clergy. Gosse maintained, "He took an absolute pleasure in the incongruity between the lofty vocation of these agents of grace and the frailties and defects of their personal conduct."

Sometimes there was a grain of malice in this and sometimes that temperamental antipathy to celibate lives noted by Burdett. But behind all this there was another attitude, more common in the Middle Ages, and still surviving in countries unaffected by the Reformation, unusual among English Catholics, least of all among converts. This is an

F*

attitude to the priesthood which treats the clergy very much as members of the family—as in such countries they often are. There is a mild type of anti-clericalism in such atmospheres, which is quite distinct from the sharper political variety, and combines this familiar attitude with a very strong determination that the priesthood should be fully worthy of its high vocation.

Very English though he was in many features, Patmore had more than a trace of this continental attitude. Perhaps the fact that his conversion, and his first and strongest impressions of Catholic life, took place in Rome had something to do with it. Older English Catholic families, which a few generations before had numbered martyrs among such priests as had been able to reach them, were hardly likely to adopt so familiar an attitude. Doubtless the English attitude had much to commend it, but historically speaking it was that of a minority, naturally changing when the clergy also became full members of a larger community. Patmore, though he was sometimes in a minority of one, never had the feelings of a minority. He was more conscious of being one in a larger community, one in an immense confluence over time and space, over history and over geography, a member of a universal church.

He was a firm believer in Tertullian's *anima naturaliter christiana,* so certain that the soul was naturally Christian that he was disposed to claim for Christianity any good wherever he found it. He thought that those who rejected revealed religion were most influenced by the denial that it was given to the whole world, "whereas it is expressly affirmed, in the very first words of St. John's gospel, that this 'Light lighteth every one that cometh into the world.'" He went on to say that "that religion has the best claims upon us which professes, as Christianity does, to be mainly a Witness of that original and universal light."

This belief also affected his view of the Church, for he wrote, "the Visible Church is like the larva of the caddis-fly, from which the winged truth shall finally emerge, perfect and beautiful, but which at present inhabits a house of singular grotesqueness." Then he recalled the shadows cast by a man in the failing light and declared, "Such a ridiculous shadow is the Visible Church of the invisible." Since early youth he had been an admirer of Plato, and there is more than a trace in this of Plato's men in the cave with their backs to the sun. Such similes had their value in pointing the contrast between this world and the other, but they were perhaps less likely to appeal to those whose task it was to diffuse light over the world. Yet Patmore was less outspoken than many mediaeval preachers in expressing the contrast between the wounds and sickness of a Church militant on earth and that other Church triumphant, having neither spot nor wrinkle.

The objection to similar criticism made by laymen is that they themselves are often more inadequate in providing examples of the religion they profess. Certainly Patmore, though he suffered much grief, had much ease and was alive to his own failings, for he wrote, "I have deserved hell, and my punishment is bliss." He was also aware that those who are most scandalised are not the most virtuous, for he even said that "holy indignation is a proof that we should do the same thing ourselves." But in answer to the general charge he stood nearer to Dr. Johnson in believing that a man should not lower his precepts to the level of his own conduct —Johnson, who recommended early rising to others, though never practising it himself, holding that in this he was at least not adding a bad precept to a bad action.

Yet, while he had his Johnsonian and therefore very English traits, his position in English letters in later life much more resembled that of a contemporary of his in France,

Barbey d'Aurevilly, who was known as the "Constable of Letters," a term that might well be applied to Patmore himself. Barbey d'Aurevilly had the same combination of religious fervour with devotion to women, though he never married and the affairs of his youth preceded his emergence as a Catholic polemist. Even in appearance the two men were much alike, the same gaunt and aloof expression reflecting their isolation and independence. Patmore was a poet, Barbey a novelist, but their essays and articles have the same tone. Barbey's remark, "I believe in the infallibility of the Pope more than in the light, for one is a principle, the other only a fact," has the ring of Patmore in it. But it is in their common independence of the ideas of their age that they were most alike. It was of Barbey that Léon Bloy said that he had a magnificence which excluded either timidity or ambition, and that he had a distinction beyond either the bourgeois or princes, in that he refused to compromise. The words could be as justly applied to Patmore.

It is true that he had never glanced at the writings of Barbey, who was quite unknown in England at that time. Indeed one of the few occasions on which he showed any knowledge of French Catholics was when a lady praised Louis Veuillot, saying that he was the greatest thinker in the world, to which Patmore drily replied that he was only the greatest in the *Universe*—which was the name of Veuillot's paper. Patmore was never at home with the French, nor with their literature. His preference went to the Spanish, whose literature, he asserted, was "great and altogether unique." Nor was it only their mystical writers, St. Teresa of Avila and St. John of the Cross, who influenced him. He greatly admired a novel of Juan Valera's, *Pepita Jiménez*, which Gosse had had translated for his International Library. The interest of this, for an understanding of Patmore, is that the novel relates the failure of a pious young aspirant to the priesthood to attain his desire, when confronted with the love of an equally pious though very human young woman. The charm of the book, and undoubtedly its attraction for Patmore, lies in the double enthusiasm with which divine and human love are presented. It is both a most religious and a most human novel. Valera's exquisite irony enables him to transform the tragedy into a comedy, in such a style that religion only gains in dignity, as the religious life is shown to demand sacrifices beyond those of which the young man is capable. But the marriage with which the book concludes has its own dignity and its own virtue: it is simply on a lower level.

Certainly this is very different from the French Jansenist type of religious novel, which is perhaps a necessary balance to French frivolity, though it is also possible that the two react disastrously on each other. The reason why Patmore was so strongly opposed both to puritanism and to frivolity was that he believed that both were equally offences against the sacred nature of human love.

This novel, *Pepita Jiménez,* aroused him to such enthusiasm that he compared Valera with Calderon in his union of "gravity of matter" with "gaiety of manner," which outside Spanish literature was only to be found in Shakespeare, and even in him "in a far less obvious degree." "It is in Spanish literature only, and without any exception," he continued, "that gaiety of life is made to appear as being not only compatible with, but the very flower of that root which in the best works of other literature hides itself in the earth, and only sends its concealed sap through stem and leaf of human duty and desire."

With the Spanish, he declared, "religion has been, as it was meant to be, a human passion." In the writings of their greatest saints and theologians, "dogma is, as it were, fused in, and becomes psychology." Whereas in "that disgusting abortion," the English religious novel, there was plenty of analysis, but no psychology, without which analysis was "merely the anatomy of a corpse."

He found in the Spanish a psychology which "deals with the personal relationships of the soul with the personalities which are above the soul, from which the soul exists, and of which the soul is the express mirror."

Patmore's intense sympathy with the Spanish mind not only illustrates his own very personal and mystical religion, but also sheds some light on his attitude towards the clergy. Too often, he felt, they were making dry expositions of doctrine, instead of burning exhortations to devotion. Once he asked a priest why he did not treat of mystical love from the pulpit as he had been discussing it with him. The answer he received was that "within a week all my congregation would be living in mortal sin." That gave him pause, and he recognised the force of the answer, which showed him that the work of the Church was to prepare the soul for divine love, which only entered those who had cleared their hearts for it, just as enduring human love only came to those who had kept themselves free from lighter passions. Increasingly he realised that the teaching of the Church was the seed of which devotion was the fruit, and that the preparation of the heart was the only road to love and perfection, whether human or divine.

Yet it remains true that his mystical approach to religion was behind his critical attitude towards ministers of the Church, which had always placed the martyrs above the mystics, demanding of its chief witnesses that they should be active in this world, not only enamoured of the other. St. Philip Neri once said that for a soul that truly loves God nothing is so difficult as simply to go on living. Patmore had something of that passionate devotion, but he did not always appreciate its further implication that earthly tasks have also to be faced, however great the temptation to concentrate wholly on the love of God. Too often he was content to dismiss the world with a lordly gesture—this was the weakness of his politics—and withdraw into mysticism. Like other mystics, he was inclined to underrate the importance of organization and ordinary pastoral work. He had a fundamental dislike of anything that was "ecclesiastical."

He declared that Gibbon's sketch of the progress of ecclesiastical history in the first three centuries was "the only piece of ecclesiastical History I have ever found interesting, or, indeed intelligible." This might appear inconsistent—apart from his obvious pleasure in praising Gibbon to upset those who did not regard him as a Christian apologist—yet it is typical of his indifference to the "ecclesiastical" element in the Church. Nobody could be less mystical than Gibbon, who therefore presented Church development as a purely administrative and proconsular affair. That pleased Patmore because he distinguished so sharply between the mystical and the administrative elements in religion. Administration was an affair for the politicians he despised. Here again he failed to allow for the essential union of body and spirit, on which he so much insisted in personal life. His was a similar confusion to that of men who speak of "the failure of the Churches" when what they really mean is the failure of mankind to produce a leader such as St. Francis of Assisi or John Wesley to revive the spirit of religion. The minister, the "ecclesiastic," is commonly blamed for not being a mystic, when it would be as just to blame the mystic for not ministering to the needs of the earth.

Between the two there is a difference of vocation, which is sometimes also an opposition. It was on the opposition that Patmore insisted. In a letter to Gosse he wrote, "All Poets and Prophets have hated Priests,—as a class,—and it has been their vocation, from the beginning, to expose 'Ecclesiasticism.'"

That was in a private letter, but he was hardly less outspoken in a published essay on Love and Poetry, a subject not closely related to this, when he claimed that poets were "wholly independent of the priests, and are often the first to discover and rebuke the lifelessness into which that order is always tending to fall."

Patmore, in his own style, was also a revivalist, seeking to give a fresh emphasis to forgotten truths. In the same essay he repeated the basis of his teaching, that "the whole of after-life depends very much upon how life's transient transfiguration in youth by love is subsequently regarded," and declared that this would be forgotten and profaned unless its sanctity was upheld by priests and poets. It was this which led to the passage quoted above in which he claimed that poets were sometimes more true to their trust.

This was the essence of the opposition he made between poet and priest, that the poet could give fresh and living words to the sacraments and the sanctity upheld by the priest. At the same time he fully accepted the authority of the priest in that province. In the Preface to *The Rod, the Root, and the Flower,* he wrote, "I make no ridiculous pretence of invading the province of the theologian by defining or explaining dogma. This I am content with implicitly accepting. . . ."

Another aspect of his attitude towards the clergy was his strong preference for regulars to seculars, partly because he had more interest in the theological studies of the religious orders than in the pastoral activities of parish priests, and partly because at that time there was a far higher standard of education among most religious orders; and it was a Jesuit, Gerard Manley Hopkins, for whom he had the greatest affection and admiration.

Any consideration of Patmore's attitude towards the clergy has to take into account his friendship with Hopkins, yet this and the letters they exchanged have an interest far beyond that. It is difficult to read these letters without having an increased respect for the characters of both men. Patmore did not meet Hopkins until 1883, on a visit to Stonyhurst, six years before the end of Hopkins' life and thirteen before the end of Patmore's much longer one. Patmore was much the older man and had his fame, yet he quickly assumed a deference to Hopkins, who spoke to him with great authority on poetry and with sympathy on religion. Patmore's battle between priest and poet was disarmed when he found them both present in one man, while Hopkins had the joy of discussing poetry with one who shared his own faith.

There is an historical oddity in this encounter between the poet of *The Angel in the House,* the first of which was published in 1854, and the poet who became one of the masters of twentieth-century verse, his poems being first published posthumously in 1918, nearly thirty years after their author's death, and achieving their greatest influence between the two World Wars. It would be hardly less odd to listen to a conversation between Tennyson and Mr. T. S. Eliot.

As recent critics have naturally paid more attention to Hopkins than to Patmore, they have as naturally tended to emphasize the difference between the two, to stress the originality of Hopkins, but this no longer requires emphasis. As the historical perspective lengthens, it is easier to see what they had in common. It is true that Patmore, while admiring certain felicities, not those which have most struck critics since, was unable to appreciate Hopkins' verse as Hopkins appreciated his, but older men are rarely able to admire verse in a younger style, while Hopkins was old enough to have outgrown the youthful habit of disparaging the immediate past, and he genuinely admired what was beyond the reach of fashion in Patmore. It is also relevant that Hopkins was closer to death than Patmore, younger only in years.

A closer reading of their letters might now cause more surprise at the extent of the sympathy between the two than wonder at their differences. The humility with which Patmore invited and accepted criticism of his own verse is also remarkable. Hopkins' criticism was searching and detailed. He made many suggestions for revision of *The Angel in the House*, which he likened to "a basket of violets," an exact image of its modest charms, even the basket, surely a small one curving outward from the base, being true to its period. Examination of the revised text shows that Patmore acted on very few of Hopkins' suggestions, but he admitted the justice of them and explained that he was beyond the writing of verse, only able to suppress or make minor emendations.

It was to Hopkins that he showed his prose work, *Sponsa Dei,* his fullest treatment of the analogies between divine and human love. What part Hopkins' criticism played in Patmore's decision to burn it has been a matter of some controversy. Hopkins, beyond questioning whether the most secret of experiences should be made public, only advised him to consult his director, as any priest might have recommended to a man with doubts. Patmore consulted Monsignor Rouse who, he said, had no strong opinions one way or the other, but thought that most of it was already stated in his verse and in papers later published in *Religio Poetae.* Alice Meynell believed that the essence of it was to be found in *The Rod, the Root, and the Flower,* published in the year before Patmore's death. Gosse, who most lamented the loss, agreed in thinking that it should not be put before all eyes and that much was already implicit in earlier work of Patmore's, chiefly regretting a fine piece of prose. Yet Patmore himself, in his last work, had come to the conclusion that disjointed fragments better expressed the highest truth than fine writing. These he published in *The Rod, the Root, and the Flower.*

Perhaps too much has been made of the incident and of the part played by others, especially Hopkins, in it, nor enough allowed for Patmore's joy in bonfires. At least it is likely that he burnt the book to please himself rather than others. Naturally those who admire his work regret the loss of any part of it, but the author may not always be the worst judge, and if Virgil's order to destroy the *Aeneid* may be cited on the other side, it is also true that he had not destroyed it himself.

It is clear that the incident had no disturbing effect on the friendship of Patmore and Hopkins, nor would either of them have viewed it in that light, even if disagreement had been greater than it was, for they were quite above the level of such childish resentment. Nor did Hopkins ever accuse Patmore of indulging himself in this or in other ways. In one of his few direct references to his character and in his only criticisms of it, he made the opposite accusation, that Patmore was lacking in what he called "tykishness," by which he understood a certain disreputable and humanising quality.

In a reference to this, Hopkins wrote: "About the 'tyke,' you did not altogether understand me. If I had said you had less than anyone else of the Bohemian, though that is not the same thing, the meaning would have been plainer. As there is something of the 'old Adam' in all but the holiest men, and in them, at least, enough to make them understand it in others, so there is an old Adam of barbarism, boyishness, wildness, rawness, rankness, the disreputable, the unrefined, in the refined and educated. It is that that I meant by tykishness (a tyke is a stray, sly, unowned dog), and said you have none of; and I did also think that you were without all sympathy for it, and must survey it when you met with it wholly from without. Ancient Pistol is the typical tyke: he and all his crew are tykes, and the tykish element undergoing dilution in Falstaff and Prince Hal appears to vanish, but of course really exists, in Henry V as king. I thought it was well to have ever so little of it, and therefore it was perhaps a happy thing that you were entrapped into the vice of immoderate smoking, for to know one yields to a vice must help to humanize and make tolerant."

This was clearly Hopkins' prose comment on what he had already said in verse: "Long live the weeds and the wilderness yet."

Certainly Patmore had more than his share of "tykishness," quite apart from smoking, but this had not come out in their correspondence owing to his deference for Hopkins, and only became clear during Hopkins' visit to Hastings.

It was precisely this human quality that most appealed to Patmore in Hopkins, on whose death he wrote that he "was the only orthodox, and as far as I could see, saintly man in whom religion had absolutely no narrowing effect on his sympathies," a remark that indicates Patmore's views no less than Hopkins' character. Just as Patmore believed that excessive puritanism led to the strangling of love by a narrow conception of duty, so he feared in all religion a tendency to confine the whole universe within a small morality of the sort which would set the Pharisee above the publican, the loveless egoist above the Magdalene. "It must be confessed," he wrote, in an essay, "Principle in Art," "that conscience makes, not only cowards, but more or less dullards, of us all." He ascribed the power of vision in children—and among men of childish mind—to their not being able to see "the flaming sword of conscience which turns every way, and hinders all men but a very few from getting a glimpse through the closed gates of Paradise." Yet it was better, he added, to be blinded by conscience than to see without it, best of all when a man of mature intellect and responsibility retained the knowledge that comes in early childhood and youth.

Behind all his thought there was this idea of primitive

revelation, of which he found traces in the pagan mysteries, in Persephone hardly less than in Psyche, for in descending to the underworld to wed the lord of Hades Persephone was also a type of the divine descent into the flesh. He made clear the connection in his mind between this and organized religion when he wrote in *The Rod, the Root, and the Flower*, "The Catholic Church alone teaches as matters of faith those things which the thoroughly sincere person of every sect discovers, more or less obscurely, for himself, but does not believe, for want of external sanction."

The truth of this relation between an inner and an outer light is a matter of general experience, for all men receive some information, however dim, from their own hearts, and there are few who do not revalue it in the light of the religion or morality obtaining in the world around them. But it is equally a matter of experience that there is a wide area of dispute between the two authorities, and it is on this battlefield, where every man who takes his religion to his heart confronts the external ministers of that religion, that the real cause of Patmore's anti-clericalism is to be found. He accepted the revealed religion taught by his clergy and he accepted the revelation of his own heart, but there was always a tension between the two, relaxed only when he found, in such men as Hopkins, a double witness of the two truths.

XI

Root and Flower

The third phase of Patmore's life, that of his third marriage, in the 'eighties and the 'nineties up to his death in 1896, was perhaps his most productive, certainly his most characteristic, for it was in those years that he became the figure which confronts posterity, the figure in the National Portrait Gallery painted by Sargent in the summer of 1894, with its erectness of carriage and its independence, with its extravagant contradictions of austerity and sensuality, acknowledging them and observing the vanishing world with a humourous droop of the left eye-lid. Maeterlinck said that it was only of the dead that portraits should be painted, as only in death were men truly themselves. Close to death, Patmore was himself.

In the achievements and in the serenity of these last years his third wife, Harriet Patmore, played an important part. At the time of his marriage to her Patmore wrote, in reply to a note of congratulation from Monckton Milnes, "You are one of the very few who can discern the seemingly obvious fact that a man probably knows his own business best in matters which concern him infinitely more than they concern anyone else." This third marriage certainly proved, as Valéry Larbaud has remarked, that the poet of marriage could not remain a widower for long. Others have accepted that fact, admitting that the third marriage was in character, but have criticized Harriet Patmore, perhaps because, while being the least attractive of the three wives, she was the one who was most aware of being Mrs. Coventry Patmore. She was in fact a famous writer's wife of a recognisable type, such as Mr. Somerset Maugham has faithfully drawn in *Cakes and Ale*. Yet the wives of other famous men, not writers, have behaved not very differently without provoking the same criticism. They too have been jealous of their husband's reputation. But the wife of a famous writer is more often criticized because she is sometimes more anxious to display him as a pillar of the established order than as an original and eccentric genius. Certainly Harriet Patmore was extremely jealous of her husband's reputation, both before and after his death, but she cannot be justly accused of having tried to show him as at all different from what he was—a task which was perhaps beyond even a wife's powers, for he was so much of a piece.

She was twice in a very awkward position, first when she was governess to his children and managing his household when Mary Patmore was an invalid, secondly after her marriage to him when she had to accept his devoted friendship with Alice Meynell. It remains an open question whether he was in love with Alice Meynell, for with a man of his temperament there was no clear borderline between love and friendship for a woman. Possibly the nearest term for his feeling is the French *amitié amoureuse,* but even that may be inaccurate. Whatever it was, it could hardly have been agreeable to Harriet Patmore, any more agreeable than it may have been even for the self-effacing Mary Patmore to know that her husband was increasingly relying on Harriet herself.

Yet Harriet Patmore behaved with dignity and moderation in these and other difficulties inevitable in dealing with a famous man, considerably older than herself, who had his own strong prejudices and stronger emotions.

The letters he wrote to her when making retreats at Ponty-pool, Pantasaph and Stonyhurst show his affection for her. "I shall be as much pleased as you can be when Saturday evening comes," he wrote. "You need not be afraid of your 'Monk' . . . returning full of severity and sourness. . . . The Church proposes, he [the Superior] says, *three* ends [in marriage], children, security from temptation, and the *cultivation of mutual love;* and this last alone brings that greatest of natural delights within the limits of even the highest Christian perfection."

On another occasion he wrote: "Francis Thompson and all the Fathers spent two hours last night in my room and we had excellent talk. Father Anselm, the Superior, and a profound contemplative, said he had never read anything so fine as the 'Precursor' [Patmore's essay on St. John the Baptist]. He and I had a long talk alone about nuptial love, and he went all lengths with me in the honour of the marriage embrace. The Fathers help me to get through my cigarettes, of which I should like to have another consignment as soon as possible."

Patmore's cigarettes were made for him at home, another responsibility which Harriet Patmore faithfully discharged.

On another retreat he wrote to her, "I mean to have a real holiday next year, that is, I mean to have you with me. I don't get any feeling of rest unless you are in the house."

This last sentence revealed his dependence on her. In the calm which she provided he had a renewal of creative power. Evidently the roots of him, still nourishing and sustaining, were in his earlier life, but they were long since far underground, buried with Emily Patmore and the two favourite children, the daughter who had borne her name and her youngest son, whose promise in youth had been no less than his father's. From that past the verse of Patmore had blossomed, but in these last years came the fruit, in a prose of a vigour and boldness which was the sum of a long life's meditations.

That these years were an Indian summer is proved by the fervour of his devotion to Alice Meynell, a figure of a later generation, but other names which occur in his correspondence over these years, from Hopkins to Gosse, who had made himself the apostle of *The Unknown Eros,* and from Robert Bridges to Francis Thompson, who hailed Patmore as his master, all were younger men, belonging more to the 'nineties and after—though Hopkins, the most modern of them, had died before then—than to the older Victorian era, for the poet of the 'fifties and *The Angel in the House* had in his third life become the friend of a new generation. Nor was he out of place in the 'nineties among the independents and eccentrics who were divided between London, Paris, and Rome, human passions, hells, and celestial visions.

This new Patmore had the prestige of his poetry behind him, but he expressed himself in prose, assembled in three books, *Principle in Art,* published in 1889, followed by *Religio Poetae* in 1893—these two were later published in one volume—and *The Rod, the Root, and the Flower,* which appeared in 1895, the year before Patmore's death, a collection of aphorisms and brief observations, hardly one more than a page in length, but containing the essence of his thought. Indeed, all his prose would go with ease into a single volume, but its content would not easily be found in a mind other than his own.

One characteristic of his prose, which has made it impossible to confine it within the limits of a separate chapter, is that the thoughts and the feelings in it not only arose from the meditations of a long life, but are in some sense a commentary on that life, for they recollect his dominating impulses, so that it has been more natural to quote many of them at different stages of this narrative—nor has it seemed

necessary to give references, as his total output of prose was
so small that those interested may find them easily enough
in the three works mentioned above.

Arthur Symons said that Patmore was "a poet of one idea
and one metre." His prose largely revolved around the same
idea, though his expression was more varied and more forc-
ible than in his verse, but the first of his three prose works,
Principle in Art, is less concerned with human and divine
love than with the nature of criticism in literature. Yet here
too his chief preoccupation shows itself, for he distinguishes
between "masculine" and "feminine" writers. For him feminine writers are those, such as Keats and Shelley, in whom
visions and emotion predominate over judgment. He implies
that most poets of the romantic revival represent the feminine principle in man, and he recalls the classical distinction
between those who were the offspring of gods with women
and those with more external splendour who sprang from
goddesses and men. The divine inspiration is no less in these,
but it is more emotional than intellectual.

The exception among the romantics, the one with the
masculine principle of judgment, was Coleridge, for whom
even from youth Patmore had the greatest respect. In Coleridge's criticism, "truth stands first and feeling second"; his
judgments have "the clearness and the finality of a mathe-
matical statement." What interested Patmore most was "the
point of rest in art," which he took from Coleridge's statement that "all harmony is founded on a relation to rest."

This "point of rest" is insignificant in itself, but the eye
turns to it for repose. In a landscape of Constable's it may
be "the sawn-off end of a branch of a tree"—or, as in one of
Michelangelo's pieces in the Sistine Chapel, "a piece of its
root." But it is most evident in Shakespeare, in whose plays
there is a figure, "the point of rest," in which the tragic
emotions or the intrigues find their balance: Kent in *King*

Lear, Friar Laurence in *Romeo and Juliet,* Horatio in *Hamlet,* Cassio in *Othello,* Bassanio in *The Merchant of Venice.*

This fertile discovery has a very wide application. Many otherwise powerful works of art fail of their effect through lack of this point of rest, for it is the sanity which is the only measure of madness. The lack of it is felt, for instance, in *Gulliver's Travels,* which failed to impress Dr. Johnson. It is a classical point, for it insists on a certain balance and moderation; it is another of the Horatian elements in Patmore. The point of rest may be trivial, or even comic, in itself—the Shakespearean fool—but it has an importance outside itself. In *Robinson Crusoe* the part is played by the parrot which at once relieves and emphasizes his isolation.

The point of rest is also to be found in sculpture. Patmore acutely observes that "an armlet, or even a finger-ring, gives every portion of the nude figure an increase of animation, unity, and repose."

But Shakespeare is always the most striking example: "Thus Horatio is the exact *punctum indifferens* between the opposite excesses of the characters of Hamlet and Laertes—over-reasoning inaction and unreasoning action—between which extremes the whole interest of the play vibrates. The unobtrusive character of Kent is, as it were, the eye of the tragic storm which rages round it. . . ."

Perhaps Patmore's most exact illustration of the point of rest is this: "A vital centre, which, like that of a great wheel, has little motion in itself, but which at once transmits and controls the fierce revolution of the circumference."

Certainly the point of rest was Patmore's most valuable contribution to criticism, for it is one of those which, once the attention has been drawn to them, remain permanently in the mind, so that it becomes a habit to apply them to any work of art.

The shrewdness of his criticism is shown by his judgments

on two novelists who in his own day had not achieved the outstanding position they now have. A friend found him reading Henry James and enquired his opinion. Patmore's reply was, "incomparably the greatest living writer of fiction." Then, when writing of woman, he quoted Hardy as "the greatest living authority on the subject," and in an essay on Pathos he had hard words for Dickens and for Dante's *Vita Nuova*—the more remarkable as he was a fervent admirer of Dante—to contrast them with "the exquisitely touching points" in Hardy's novels.

Of his other literary essays one of the most interesting is on Alice Meynell. When she was at the height of her fame, Sir Max Beerbohm said that eulogies of her from Coventry Patmore or George Meredith were hardly to be avoided in the press, but in this essay, though Patmore refers to her as "a woman of genius" and "one of the very rarest products of nature and grace," he declared that she had not enough of the "feminine factor," which made the greatness of Keats and Shelley, to be counted among the classical poets. For him these masculine and feminine factors were independent of the writer's sex. He quoted the whole of "Renouncement," and declared that it was "almost faultless," only to add that, compared with what was classical in Herrick or Crashaw, it was "as moonlight unto sunlight." But he judged her prose to be more classical, having "the marriage of masculine force of insight with feminine grace and tact of expression."

He always looked for the personality behind the written work. He found this in Alice Meynell, but in coming to know her he recognised how much more there was to her than her light and sensitive essays and poems, a certain charm and delicate power which extended beyond her work, witty and perceptive though much of this was.

In this she was truly classical, more in the line of Jane Austen than the Brontës, always dominating her inspiration, never driven by it. Her effect on Patmore was intoxicating. She really extended the range of his perceptions, which came to him chiefly through women, because she was a woman he had never met before, indeed a woman who had never existed before. What Gosse did in making his work known to the younger generation, she did in making the younger generation known to him.

In 1891 he had been obliged to leave Hastings, owing to the lapse in the lease of his house, and he had gone to one in a backwater at Lymington, where he was to die five years later. From 1891 to 1894 he sometimes went to London, visiting the Meynells at Palace Court, and they also stayed with him at Lymington. With them he was always an honoured guest, but it was inevitable that their meetings should mean much more to him, who lived in isolation with his work behind him, than to Alice Meynell, who had a vital family life, a journalistic life, and a social life, besides her personal life. Apart from anything else, she had not time fully to respond to his devotion, even if that had been her desire.

Certainly she understood and admired him, perhaps uniquely. Very exactly she expressed the feeling of her own gift towards his: "The compassion of the slighter acquaintance with sorrow for the greater, and of the smaller capacity for the vaster, is a remorse of tenderness, lowliness, and respect. . . ."

She was felicitous. This felicity of praise from a charming and intelligent woman had an effect on Patmore's years similar to that of wines as heady on a young man. He was passionately grateful, and all his passions centred on love, and she was a woman.

When men exceed in their emotions, it falls to women to limit them. Both he and she were better writers than talkers, and there was an ease in their correspondence which could not always be recaptured in conversation. But they ceased to meet before the last two years of his life.

Clearly it was impossible for her to support so passionate a friendship. She was irreproachable, and there is sometimes a moment when a woman has also to be unapproachable. It is possible that hers was a nature which kept a greater distance than was necessary, for she later reproached herself for her "failure of love to those that loved me." But that was her character, for which she was loved.

Patmore's admiration for her continued unbounded. To some this has seemed the folly of an old man, but that again is perhaps to assume too much. She was worthy of his devotion, and his work was worthy of her respect. It was one of those situations which do not occur in the lives of men with a nice regard for the appearance of their emotions or with a self-conscious pride. In a sense it was more like Patmore's first hopeless love for Miss Gore in the Place Vendôme. Some lives, like some epics, end where they began, inscribing a full circle, young men dreaming dreams and old men seeing visions which are substantially the same.

This is all very well, but Patmore's last passion was not exempt from the frailties of human love. He was painfully jealous of Alice Meynell's friendship for George Meredith and spoke sadly of his being supplanted in her regard. His petulant silence on being denied a conversation with her has been recorded by Mrs. Belloc Lowndes. He behaved with all the folly which is more easily forgiven in a young than in an old man. In short, he behaved like a lover—but it is doubtful whether he knew how else to behave, for he had only lived under the impulse of human and divine passions, and this was only the last example in his life of the tension between the two.

He spoke of its being impossible to live long "without delight" and said that he was waiting "somewhat impatiently" for death. He was fortunate, for he had not long to wait.

He had the sort of vitality which is impatient for consummation in every sphere, the sort that was once responsible for cutting off the ear of a high priest's servant—exactly the gesture to appeal to Patmore.

This same irritable old man had in 1893 published his *Religio Poetae,* a short and unequal collection of twenty-one essays, of which the first treats of poetry, the voice of natural love, and religion, while the last three turn again to human and divine love, the last of all, "Dieu et Ma Dame," summarising his life's meditations on this subject, perhaps in a form not very different from the lost *Sponsa Dei.*

The title-essay, "Religio Poetae," claims that the poet is a visionary whose likenesses are "truly the visible *ultimates* of the unseen," for it is only from these ultimate rays of the divine sun that men can trace the source of light. Patmore quotes a remark of Goethe's, that "God is manifested in ultimates," adding that this is "a doctrine destined to produce some amazing developments of Christianity, which is yet in its infancy, though it seems, as it has always seemed to contemporaries, to be in its decay." The poet is closest to reality: "All realities will sing, but nothing else will."

In the work of the greatest theologians, from St. Augustine to St. John of the Cross, the amount of this reality is "ten times greater" than "in all the poets of the past two thousand years put together." But this is in a region beyond poetry: "Its realities take away the breath which would, if it could, go forth in song."

The future development of Christianity will lead the natural feelings and instincts, glorified by the poet, into this higher region. This may be the Holy Spirit's fulfilling of Christ, as Christ fulfilled the Father worshipped by the Israelites. "Our Lord, by an intervention which He declared to be premature, converted water into the wine of the Marriage Feast." But it may no longer be premature, Patmore implies, when marriage is more truly seen as a stage towards divine love.

This too is all very well, but the cynic looking back on Patmore's life or on his devotion to Alice Meynell, closer to the moment when he wrote these lines, may miss that "inexhaustible source of joy" which he called "too grave for smiles." No doubt this particular stone has to be thrown; the question, as before, is who is to throw it. Patmore was not a model of perfection, but it is likely that his passions would have been stormier if they had been based on a less perfect ideal than the one he set before him. The lowering of moral standards since his day has not noticeably improved behaviour in such matters. It is true that men are less hypocritical, but the loss of hypocrisy has also been the loss of effort, and it may be that hypocrisy is a necessary reticence in moral conflicts.

Having stated in *Religio Poetae* that the natural affections may be transformed into divine love as water into wine, Patmore naturally goes on to consider St. John the Baptist, the Precursor of Christ as natural love is the precursor of the divine. "His baptism was necessary even to Christ as the representative of Christians, for none can receive effectually Christ's baptism of fire and the Holy Spirit without the previous baptism of the purifying water of natural love." So the Baptist says, "He must increase, I must decrease," for natural love only prepares the way for the divine which passes immeasurably above it. "The flower is not for the seed, but the seed for the flower."

That is why John the Baptist was so often shown by the old painters as the companion of the Christ Child with the Madonna. Theology has considered the Baptist as here representing the old dispensation, the last figure of the Old Testament, the last successor of Melchisedec, giving place to the new, but Patmore always tended to equate the old dispensation with "the Child's dream," the primitive revelation to the childhood of mankind reproduced in the individual child, so that natural religion and natural affection had for him a similar origin.

Patmore's next essay is on the "Language of Religion," which conceals truths in rites, myths, and parables, obeying the command, "Tell not the vision to any man till Christ be risen" in him. Yet some men of simple faith in Little Bethel and Sion chapels "use the obscurest imagery of Scripture with an evident grasp of significance which many a Bishop might have envied." This is because such veiled truths are clear to those who have preserved their sense of primitive revelation. All myths had a hidden meaning for Patmore, who would have agreed with Professor Toynbee's saying that "mythology is an intuitive form of apprehending and expressing universal truths."

Patmore even claimed that certain images and rites often illuminated the Church's doctrine better than words. He was particularly impressed by the Egyptian obelisk in Rome which stands in so direct a relation to St. Peter's. Considering its inscription, "Lion of the Tribe of Judah," he explains that this came out of Egypt, which is an image for Nature. The obelisk's significance is that Egypt, or Nature, "is become Christ" by taking on "the body which, without Him, is Egypt." This was one of Patmore's favourite images, and his own tomb in the cemetery at Lymington is surmounted by an obelisk.

Another essay, "The Bow Set in the Cloud," admits that there may be surprise at the assumption that "some knowledge of Christian mysteries has been enjoyed by individuals in all times and places," but it is to be remembered that "the Incarnation was an act done in eternity as well as time . . . nor do glimpses of the heavenly vision seem to have been

G

absolutely denied to any race of men." Patmore adds that "the anthropomorphic character, which so universally marks the religion of the simple" and is a cause of scandal to the sophisticated, may be regarded "as a remote confession of the Incarnation." This is his central idea, one more affirmation of the primitive revelation made to all mankind, collectively in universal religion, individually in "the Child's dream."

In the same essay he also mentions another idea essential to his thought: "Man *(homo),* according to the writer of Genesis, originally contained the woman." In the regenerated state the *homo* will *be* a marriage, combining the feminine and the masculine natures, the feminine increased in its receptivity and response, yet without protest against masculine strength and wisdom—the protest which is the cause of all disorder. The blindness of an ancient prophet came from the same vision "which blinded him, as it does any one who has beheld it, to all other objects of sight." It also followed for Patmore that perfect virginity was a reconciliation of the two natures in one body.

The Redeemer encompassed by a woman in the Incarnation was the highest image of this reconciliation.

In most of these essays of *Religio Poetae* there is some insight, not originality—Patmore always disclaimed that—but his own vehement attempt to reconcile the religious insights of all ages, no less vehement than his effort to reconcile the passions and perceptions of his own life. Some of these essays have already been considered in his political views and in his attitude towards the clergy; of the rest, the most substantial are the last three in the book.

The first of these three, "Love and Poetry," begins with the statement: "Every man and woman who has not denied or falsified nature knows, or at any rate feels, that love, though the least 'serious', is the most significant of all things."

The unreasonableness of love is a main cause of its power,

"for who but a 'scientist' values greatly or is greatly moved by anything he can understand—that which can be comprehended being necessarily less than we are ourselves?" This remark is very typical of Patmore, whose truculence, provoked by some provincial assertions of Victorian scientists, did not obscure a real shrewdness, for he here pierced to the central dogma of that rationalist age, that the mind of man was the measure of the universe. For him man, so far from being the judge of creation, was the lowest creature capable of perceiving the spirits above him—and that only through "the smoked glass of humanity."

Having emphasized the mystery of love, he admitted that it was rooted deeper in the earth than any other passion, but for that reason like "the Tree Igdrasil, soars higher into heaven." Its roots were therefore of decisive significance in every life, for "the whole of after-life depends very much upon how life's transient transfiguration in youth by love is subsequently regarded." Patmore went on to claim that married love "bears the clearest marks of being nothing other than the rehearsal of a communion of a higher nature." The poet was its prophet, and it was his task to convey "without any flavour of cant or exclusiveness, the graces which the chosen people have too often denied or disgraced in their eyes." This last remark was a dig at the timidity of his fellow-Christians and particularly his fellow-Catholics.

The next essay, on woman, is a lighter piece, in which he begins by welcoming the higher education of women. So long as she abstained from "absolute outrages against nature—such as divided skirts, free-thinking, tricycles, and Radicalism—neither Greek, nor conic sections, nor political economy, nor cigarettes, nor athletics" could do anything but enhance her charm. The contrast is comic, yet even today it may shed some light on the difference between a traditional idea of womanhood and a more modern version. What Patmore had in mind was the necessary contrast between the sexes, for though he admitted that "no man should be without some touch of womanhood, and no woman without some manhood," he vigorously denied that there could be any equality between them. "When man becomes womanish," woman tries "all sorts of hopeless tricks—the most hopeless of all being that of endeavouring to become manly—in order the better to attract him who has become womanish." There was something prophetic in this. Patmore foresaw the masculinisation of women and he placed the blame for it squarely upon men—"it is wholly the man's fault." He added that "no right-minded woman would care a straw for her lover's adoration if she did not know that he knew that after all he was the true divinity." When order is preserved, "by becoming the slave of his reason she reduces him to a like captivity to her desires." In fact Patmore was so little in sympathy with equality between men and women that he could only discuss their relations in terms of slavery and captivity —on both sides.

The final essay is "Dieu et Ma Dame." To a man, Patmore claims, this phase "is no irreverent or hyperbolic legend for his double but not divided worship." The ideal womanhood has only once been fully realised, but "every woman seems to be capable of more or less representing" this to some man, at least for a moment. So woman is to man "the Priestess of the Divine Truth or Beauty to him, as he is Priest of the Divine Love or Power to her."

Patmore then proceeds to give examples of the analogies between divine and human love, of which the first is the mystery of choice, "the way of a man with a maid" being as incomprehensible as the way of God with a soul. There is also the same consciousness of being unique in being loved, which produces not pride but humility, because it is the creation of love. In both loves past corruptions are forgotten:

"the seed of Divine Love and the seed almost divine of a pure and fervid mortal affection" transform "many a Magdalen, the just envy of many who were always pure."

In both loves the lover complains, as to Martha, when the beloved puts housework above the direct love of him. Both loves require a belief in his love, a belief which alone can make her rise above herself.

In both there is no equality: "she delights in calling herself his slave; he delights in being hers . . . captivity to the beloved animates either kind of love—if, indeed, they be not really one in kind."

Then there is the reciprocal desire of "the great for the small and the small for the great . . . to a great man and to a God a little love is a great thing."

In both loves there is a longing to die for the beloved— "I have longed for this hour. . . ."

In both the least inattention seems a mortal offence, for only perfection satisfies.

In both the misery of temporary separation seems eternal.

Both loves explain the beloved to herself, giving her "the destined complement of her being, and the key to her unintelligible dreams."

In both there is "the coexistence of a celestial and exceedingly virginal pride with an insatiable appetite for its surrender and sacrifice."

Patmore concludes: "The last of the innumerable analogies, or rather identities, which I shall here notice is the indissolubility of union, when it has reached its final stage."

It is clear that the view of love here put forward demands inequality as its basis, yet one equality in men and women Patmore admitted, "each being equally, though not alike, a manifestation of the Divine to the other." Again and again he insisted that "the phenomena of the human relationship of love are such because they are the realities of the Divine.

For all properly human instincts are no other than the lineaments of God. . . ."

This was his last essay. In the 'eighties he had written a number of articles which Frederick Greenwood, one of his closest friends whom he greatly admired for standing consistently above the current of the age, had published in the *St. James's Gazette*. When this failed for lack of support there was some question of a paper aimed at a wider public, and Patmore seriously suggested the *Twopenny Damn* as a title. This project was not realised, but it shows that he was eager for a chance to write more publicly. Other articles of his were published by Frank Harris, who again was hardly a withdrawn character, in the *Fortnightly Review*. Patmore made use of these articles in compiling *Principle in Art* and *Religio Poetae*.

In his backwater at Lymington, and especially after the end of his visits to the Meynells in London, Patmore became more remote from the world. But his preoccupations did not change and his personal optimism persisted: as in his last visits to London he had "never heard better talk in my life," so the isolated lodge at Lymington was "the finest estate in Hampshire." So his son's poems, his daughter's drawings, his own pups, had always been the finest that ever were. In the same spirit he was able to declare in 1894 that he was "better than he had ever been in his life."

Certainly that applied to his work, whatever was true of the aged frame now creaking towards the cemetery, for in the following year, the one before his death, he published *The Rod, the Root, and the Flower*, which is in some sense his masterpiece, for if, as Gosse said, the most striking thing about him was that he was "exceedingly unlike other men," this was exceedingly unlike other books, and it is sometimes uniqueness, even more than excellence, which confers immortality.

This small book has four sections, "Aurea Dicta," of which some are no more than a line, "Knowledge and Science," "Homo," and "Magna Moralia," consisting of paragraphs very few of which run over a small page, the average being around a dozen lines.

In the preface Patmore said that he sincerely rejoiced that some found his writings "damned good to steal from," "not knowing the sources from which I also have derived my matter—and make it my only claim to be heard that I have done so."

It is true that there is sometimes an archaic quality in his sayings, for they evoke the same surprise as a line in an early Egyptian poem or a phrase from some remote myth. His preoccupations were always primitive, and some of the most striking lines in the book are those which throw light on ancient myths, as this: "Rhea, the Earth, was the mother of the Gods, and it is only by inspired knowledge of our own nature, or earth, which is seen, that we can know anything of the Divine, which is unseen."

Other of the "Aurea Dicta" depend perhaps too much on a response from the reader. Others have a truth which echoes all legends and all experience as, "The promises of the Devil are kept to the letter and broken in the spirit; God's promises are commonly broken to the letter and fulfilled past all hope to the spirit," which simply emphasizes that deception is in material things and satisfaction only in the spirit, a truth of general experience—but it is memorably and boldly expressed. Patmore had a gift for sharp distinction, as in this, "Science is a line, art a superficies, and life, or the knowledge of God, a solid."

The "Aurea Dicta," as most such aphorisms, are unequal. There is a dull page or two, then suddenly two of the best come together. "In times of darkness and temptation the influx of blessing from God is not stopped but only checked in its course, as by a dam, and the longer the temptation the greater the flood of good that pours in. . . ." This observation is followed by one even more penetrating. Patmore quotes, "To him that waits all things reveal themselves," then adds, "provided that he has the courage not to deny, in the darkness, what he has seen in the light," one of the most useful sayings in the entire book.

A page or two later comes a saying inscribed on his tomb: "All the love and joy that a man has ever received in perception is laid up in him as the sunshine of a hundred years is laid up in the bole of the oak." This truth, held in an exact image, is perhaps even stronger than Browning's "Rabbi Ben Ezra" in its promise of wisdom to old age, going far to justify Patmore's belief that a fortunate epigram may be more effective than verse in dealing with the highest realities.

All his best sayings are affirmations, usually joyous. Bonald said, "We have no need of masters to teach us how to doubt." It is certainly not for doubts that one goes to Patmore. That is his limitation, for there is a value in doubt and anguish, as in suffering, without which the fountain of pity is often reduced to a feeble trickle. But mankind also needs a master to affirm "the negative and transient nature of pain and sorrow and the eternal character of joy."

In making such affirmations Patmore was often closer in spirit to primitive religion than to later Christian thinkers, and closer to the catacombs with their "Good Shepherd" than to a later emphasis on the Crucifixion.

He was also, in opposition to some contemporary Christians, more interested in heaven than in hell. Another of the "Aurea Dicta" states, "Heaven becomes very intelligible and attractive when it is discerned to be—Woman." Osbert Burdett illuminates this by relating it to a later saying which defines heaven as "the synthesis of absolute content and infinite desire," which, he adds, "might almost stand for a definition of love." Patmore so telescoped his thought that much of it needs such reference to its other expressions, but even his most obscure sayings have some light in them which reference or meditation will reveal.

On the same subject he declared that whatever form "the unknown felicity" may take, "it must include all the felicity and fidelity of limitation to which we now cleave." That was always one of his chief efforts, to point out, as to Bunyan's man bowed over his muck-rake, the heavenly light which was ignored.

Some of his sayings also serve as a criticism of his own philosophy, as, "Heaven is too much like Earth to be spoken of as it really is, lest the generality should think it like their Earth, which is Hell," which explains why his views on marriage have not been more generally accepted, for it may be that only those who have shared his joy can share his vision.

Constantly he affirms the necessity for natural roots: "Religion has no real power until it becomes *natural*," and, "The power of the Soul for good is in proportion to the strength of its passions." So, he adds, "great Saints have often been great sinners."

A few of the sayings are sharp, but the most perceptive gain from this, which proves that there is no weakness in their breadth: "It is the privilege of the simple and pure to know God when they see Him. All men have seen God, but nearly all call Him by a very different name. The light shineth in darkness, but the darkness comprehendeth it not."

Patmore was able to treat words and thoughts in a style which ran naturally into a Scriptural quotation—not a common gift.

The second section of *The Rod, the Root, and the Flower,* which is "Knowledge and Science," is both less pointed and less brilliant than the "Aurea Dicta." These paragraphs show Patmore as more akin to the present age than to his own

G*

in being more interested in psychology than in physical science, the passion of his contemporaries, who put mechanics before mathematics, straining to reduce the universe to a working model as their successors have constricted truth to complex equations. His main reproach to nineteenth-century science was simply its preoccupation with the material surface of the universe, the superficial, and its neglect of those psychological depths which were of greater value to mankind.

It is characteristic of him that when he seized on a psychological truth it was often one most abhorrent to his contemporaries, such as that revealed in Abraham's attempt to sacrifice Isaac. A man could only rise above himself, he declared, by offering up his first-born, his dearest possession, his "ruling love." He had actually to lift the knife—"not so much to prove his sincerity to God as to himself; for no man who has not thus won assurance of himself can advance surely." Only then would he find that he had killed a ram and that his dearest wish was safe; he would also realise why the place of the sacrifice was named "the land of vision."

The third section, "Homo," is again concerned with the Incarnation and divine love. Patmore argues that the body with its two sides, its two consciences, rational and emotional, its heart with a double and contrasted action, and its many other dualisms, has been formed for two persons, yet has "a unity arising from cooperation which makes the body itself as clear an echo of the Trinity as the soul is." So, he says, the Catholic Church insists on its sanctity, because it "alone of all Churches teaches the Incarnation as a present reality."

Earlier religious ideas are also to be found in the nature of man, who is Mount Olympus, "so long as he confesses that he is nothing in himself," and in him are "the powers and majesties, beauties and beatitudes of all Gods and Goddesses."

Patmore considered that the originators of the ancient myths were the "true psychologists," and there was some heavenly significance in the joining of Vulcan to Venus, Gods to women, and men to Goddesses.

"Magna Moralia," the fourth and last section of *The Rod, the Root, and the Flower*, has most unity, being dominated by the theme of the "ruling love," which must first be sacrificed, but then becomes the rule of the spiritual life. Patmore's thought is often in line with Jesuit devotion—this section includes a quotation from St. Ignatius—and he was received into the Church by a Jesuit, while another Jesuit, Hopkins, was the priest he most admired. He also had an instinctive sympathy for the Spanish religious temperament. It seems likely in fact that the Jesuit line of his thought was more natural than due to direct influence, for he had both a Jesuit breadth and a Jesuit austerity. He was also in such constant reaction against the Reformation that this naturally aligned him with the chief force of the Counter-Reformation.

In "Magna Moralia" he emphasizes that "virtues are nothing but ordered passions, and vices nothing but passions in disorder." Happy is the man who has conquered his passions, "but far happier he whose servants and friends they have become." Patmore also notes that in the spiritual combat no struggle is really unsuccessful, for to go on fighting "after repeated disgrace and failure *is* victory over the three enemies of the soul, Sloth, Pride and Despair."

"Happy is he who understands the mystery of Persephone," (who had descended into the underworld, yet returned to the light of heaven), Patmore quotes, "over such an one Hades has no power." God is the only reality, and Hades is the realm of shades and phantoms. "All evils are phantoms, even physical pain, which a perfectly courageous heart converts, by simply confronting it, into present and sensible joy of purgation and victory."

Constantly in these paragraphs he recalls that each individual has his "ruling love," which has a part to play in humanity: "each Soul is safely led by her own desires, which God gives her back glorified directly she has made a sincere sacrifice of them." But they have to be sacrificed with full sincerity: "We have, with the 'Wise Man,' to leave our own people," before seeing the Incarnate God, and afterwards are told to "go back *another way, into our own country.*"

Patmore points out that there is a necessity not only in this sacrifice, but in the darkness of divine love which would seem horrible, monstrous and chaotic unveiled before the undiscerning: "The hideousness of some of the images worshipped by those among the ancients who best understood the Gods was not without its meaning."

The book concludes with a final blast against the puritanism of the Reformation which has "nearly killed" the Catholic Church with its infection, so that human love, precursor of the divine, has been branded with impurity. But, Patmore prophesied, it was "about to be enthroned in Catholic psychology as it never was before."

An appendix to *The Rod, the Root, and the Flower* contains lines found among his papers after his death, some of them in no way inferior to the "Aurea Dicta." One of the sharpest notes "the enthusiasm for goodness which shows that it is not the habit of the mind"—perhaps a note prompted by some of the pious chatter which so irritated him. Another returns to the anguish and horror which are a necessary counter-balance to the felicity and freedom of heaven, as the way of the Cross is the only route to heaven: "In the crucified seraph St. Francis saw the only recorded vision of the state of the Blessed in Christ."

One of the most interesting comments on *The Rod, the Root, and the Flower* was made by Sir Herbert Read when he said that it was "not wholly ridiculous" to compare it with

Pascal's *Pensées*. This is certainly a most fertile comparison, for quite apart from the relative merits of the two works the men themselves become clearer in the light of the contrast which, between Christians, could hardly be greater, for Pascal's Jansenism was at the opposite pole from Patmore's strong reaction against puritanism, Jansenism and all such limitations of the human and the natural, further emphasized by Patmore's liking for the Jesuits and Pascal's detestation of them.

It has been plausibly urged that Pascal's *Pensées* are among the greatest of apologetic works, providing an almost unique introduction to Christianity. Pascal himself went through a conversion in the Protestant sense of that term— he "saw the light," dating everything from his conversion, and his "Memorial," constantly with him, was his passport into a new world. Consequently he is the best of guides to those on the same route. Patmore went through no such dramatic experience; oddly, it is he who gives far more the impression of being a born Catholic. Consistently his emphasis was always on the most Catholic aspects of the religion he shared with Pascal, not those emphasized by Pascal himself, who mentioned neither the Mother of God nor the Eucharist, basic to Patmore's thought. If Pascal was concerned to show "the misery of man without God," Patmore, meditating on the Incarnation, was struck by the greatness of God in man. In fact, while Pascal is always on his knees before the crucifix, Patmore is kneeling with the oxen before his God made man.

Here the greatness of Pascal throws a strong light on Patmore's weakness. Always to Patmore, whatever emphasis he laid on sacrifice, there clings some of the ease and comfort found in his own century and in his own life. Of the many ways that lead to the many mansions of heaven he did not often tread that which goes over rocks under a darkened sky.

Against his many meditations on the Incarnation and the Mother of God, only one or two so much as mention the Crucifixion. At times his attitudes almost recalls that of Clovis, who said that if he had been there with his Franks it would never have happened. One of his few references to the Crucifixion, in the penultimate paragraph of *The Rod, the Root, and the Flower,* says that "the real and innermost sacrifice of the Cross was the consummation of the descent of Divinity into the flesh." In other words the Crucifixion was the Incarnation, and he at once returned to meditate on this.

Traditional Christianity has a different view. "Ave Crux, spes unica" remains the aptest summary of its central inspiration. There Pascal was more at one with the Christians of all ages.

Yet Patmore too was in a great tradition. It is natural that he, the patriarch, should have laid his first emphasis on natural religion and found in pre-Christian sources figures of the coming revelation, natural too that he should express the serenity of the catacombs, that strange serenity which, closer to the Crucifixion, at times seemed almost to overlook the agony in joy that God had been born into the world, natural that he should be more at home in the Middle Ages than in the divided world of the Reformation. Constantly he referred to the Reformation almost as if it was a personal tragedy in his own life, as in a sense it was, for it divided his intensely English character from the bulk of his fellow-countrymen. It was not only the puritanism of the Reformation that he disliked, particularly resenting the inroads it had made upon his own Church, but the division it made in religious life, the breaking up of the rainbow which was the divine witness to the universal light. The quickness and generosity of his sympathy with those outside his own communion was also a protest against the Reformation.

Here again the contrast with Pascal, a man on whom the Reformation had left its mark, is apparent. Pascal's reason was opposed to Patmore's vision, for it is more true to say of Pascal, in opposition to his own often ineptly quoted saying, that in him reason created emotions stronger than the heart's; while for Patmore "all reasoning ends in an appeal to self-evidence."

Yet Sir Herbert Read was surely right to claim for *The Rod, the Root, and the Flower* a place not far below Pascal's *Pensées;* for them both may be used the words which Patmore applied to Plato: "A man may read Plato without clearly comprehending much of what he means. He cannot read him without becoming, in some degree, a changed man."

XII

The Independent

Edmund Gosse, a mandarin of established English life and librarian to the House of Lords, used strange phrases in writing of Coventry Patmore, whom he described as being "like a king in exile," and again "like the Phoenix of fable, the solitary specimen of an unrelated species." More than once Gosse referred to him as "this extraordinary man." Frank Harris, an extreme contrast to Gosse's respectable and established figure, was no less struck by Patmore's unique distinction. For him Patmore "represented all that was best in English life," though he was "a mass of contradictions because at odds with his time." Having visited his home, Harris found him "lovable and beloved by his own even to reverence."

That Patmore had such effects on men as different as Gosse and Harris is one illustration of the strength and independence in his character, striking even to those out of sympathy with his ideas. Yet he can hardly appear what is called a sympathetic character to those who set no value on his ideas or to those who find them repugnant, for these ideas were too closely interwoven in the fabric of his life and in the stuff of his being. Even his weaknesses and his failures can only be judged in relation to them, for they produced the tensions between his passions and his perceptions of the other world.

It is to his advantage then that his were universal ideas,

not limited by time or climate, going back to the most primitive of religious conceptions, extending from the suburbs of North London to the islands of the South Seas. His wisest critic, Valéry Larbaud, found in him "those eternal ideas which dominate the centuries, which are like salt preserving all things; a harmonious balance between instinct and human reason, respect for the body and an accurate perception of what is material—a sort of moral mathematics." He concluded by saying that he found in him something of what Patmore called "that peace which surpasses—that is to say, is more intelligent than—all understanding."

It is true that in all his affirmations Patmore looked towards peace and in all his tensions never forgot that life is "joy itself." Though moments of perfect sunshine may be brief, he wrote, "the joy of life will not be wholly obscured to us by any external evil, provided the breast is clear of remorse, envy, discontent, or any other habitually cherished sin." It is characteristic of him that he numbered discontent, that fretting against the laws of life which is the romantic disease, among such sins. Life became gay, he declared, as it mounted towards the heights: "The profound spiritualities of the Greek and Indian myths laugh for joy; and there are, perhaps, no passages in Scripture more fondly dwelt upon in the Roman Breviary than those which paint the gladness of the Uncreated Wisdom." Then he quoted the famous passage: "When he balanced the foundations of the earth, I was with him, forming all things: and was delighted every day, playing before him at all times, playing in the world: and my delight is to be with the children of men."

This delight is outside time, but it is possible that such quotations are less pleasing to the religious temper of this restless and anxious age than to that of the last century. Yet Patmore was quite pessimistic enough about the trend of history. The more a man knows about the past, he maintained, "the less he will be inclined to believe that the world is making any advances towards the realisation of the promise which every age repeats." For life contained "scarcely anything for fruition, but abundance for hope." But that hope was in the other world. On worldly optimism Patmore's comment was: "The rejoicings of Lord Macaulay and his like over the recent advances of mankind are exactly those of a prosperous shopman over the increase of his business."

On such matters he could be as pessimistic as a generation brooding on bombs. His optimism was wholly interior, based on a grateful mind, which he once described as rising only from "a heart that loves God."

It was this sense of grateful dependence on God which produced his independence towards the world. No doubt this independence was also in his temperament, but it was formed and developed by personal experience, owing little to the age in which he lived. Gosse wrote of him: "He thought in hyperbole, and nothing was moderate or mediocre with him. If he approved of a person, that person walked along the mountain tops, with the light of God upon his face. He disapproved, and the man became not merely a failure, a poor creature, but a positive cretin, a blot upon the face of nature."

This free vent he gave to his emotions, his fervent egoism, were the natural expression of his independence. If there is increasing uniformity in the contemporary world, with its single parties and its large groupings which insist on a solid front hardly less oppressive, this may not be so much due to dullness of mind or a dead level of opinion as to the lack of strong emotions, which are the creators of independence, whether they spring from love of life, of family, or of country.

Such deep attachments create independence because they are natural growths. They are further strengthened if they are rooted in a religion which has so entered the heart that it has become, as Patmore said, "natural". "You can best move this world," he wrote, "by standing and making it clear that you stand upon another." It was on this stand that he based his independence.

He believed that this religion on which he took his independent stand was human and universal, natural to man, being, as he never tired of repeating, "the light that lighteth every man coming into the world," natural as love of life, of family, or of country. It had to satisfy the demands of reason, but it was above reason as love was above reason, and it only became fully natural when it was introduced by love into the heart, for its central truth to him was that God so loved the world as to descend into the human body.

The essence of man's freedom, the basis of his independence, was that he was free to accept or reject God, consequently to decide in what sort of world he was going to live, for the light of nature was the human eye, which opened in each man on a fresh vision of the world—and the universe itself.

There was a savage individualism in this which could be pushed to the verge of insanity and even beyond it, for the madman, of all men, lives most in a world of his own. Such an individual outlook has then to be checked by the reason and experience of others, but without this individual outlook it is difficult to see what freedom remains to a man: if he cannot decide in what world he is going to live, he can only be a slave to the ideas of others. That is what Patmore meant when he said, "Great is his faith who dares believe his own eyes."

In this century freedom has received more tributes than ever before. There has been public debate on every sort of freedom, economic, political, religious. Yet there has not been a corresponding increase in independence of mind. Here it is material to recall a paper once read by the Spanish

philosopher, Eugenio d'Ors, to the International Congress of
Philosophy, in which he argued that freedom could not be
qualified, because it was the first movement of the human
spirit, a substantive, not an adjective. This is, in fact, the
basic freedom, the individual vision of the world, and it is
precisely this which has most diminished in an age where
every aspect of knowledge is decided by the authority of
specialists, in whom knowledge may sometimes limit vision
no less than experience may often stifle love. In politics
there are systems and theories in the mind, instead of pity
and the brotherhood of man in the heart; in religion apolo-
getics take precedence over meditation, and the presence of
God is more often demonstrated than revealed in daily life.
Only the artist who, as Patmore maintained, is in permanent
protest against authority, defends his individual vision, while
the young turn to other worlds revealed by a fictitious science, because an unimaginative education has suppressed
their individual vision of this one.

Yet without vision the people perish, and independence
dies in nations no less than in individuals, as it is only their
common vision which preserves the individuality of nations.

In the determination with which he preserved his independence Patmore proved his loyalty to the first vision of
his life, that which he received from his first love in Paris,
deciding his vocation as the poet of marriage.

In his insistence on this vision, no less than in the importance he assigned to primitive religion, he recalls another
great independent who came after him, D. H. Lawrence.
They were alike in their campaigns against puritanism and
in their insistence on an emotional response to the universe. Lawrence quoted St. Augustine's saying that God created the world afresh every morning, to add that to the living, emotional soul this was true; and his *Movements in
European History* he came near to Patmore's "light that

lightens every man" by declaring that every age had its light. In the last century, he said, it was reduced to a small and "rather ghastly" flicker, but "it never went out." At the end of his life Lawrence, in "A Propos of Lady Chatterley's Lover" also came nearer to Patmore's views on marriage, for in this he wrote that, when the priest said, "If you marry, you marry for ever," the people "accept the decree, the doom, and the dignity of it."

It was emotional force in Lawrence, no less than in Patmore, which generated his independence, leading him, like Patmore, to find in the simplest religious convictions a similar force of which the world stood permanently in need, for in the essay just quoted he also wrote that "belief is a profound emotion that has the mind's connivance."

In this he strangely approached a remark made by Patmore's son Henry in one of his letters. Henry Patmore wrote: "Facts ought if possible to be made to yield to feeling. For facts are only material *things* and *feelings* are a part of our souls." Here, too, he showed that almost "psychical phenomenon" noted by Richard Garnett of producing what can only be called an "original echo" of his father's ideas.

It is evident that strength of emotion alone is an inadequate guide to truth, but it is hardly less evident that no truth can be productive unless it has strong emotion behind it. The tension between faith and reason marks a deeper tension between reason and feeling, that exists in every man, for the world disagrees less about facts than about the degree of emotional emphasis to be put upon them. It was in the intensity of the emphasis that he placed on the fact of love, not in any fresh discovery, that Coventry Patmore asserted his independence of those for whom the same fact had a limited biological and social significance.

This intensity he maintained until the end of his life, though towards the end he grew a little impatient to reach

that homeland to which his vision of love looked for com-
pletion. His gaunt frame had come to have almost the look
of a skeleton, in preparation for that change. The lung
trouble which had persisted all his life, fixing on him when
he was weakest in his grief at the death of his first wife,
finally showed in bronchial disease, though it was a colic
which was destined to end him. Yet even in the last summer
of his life, that of 1896, he wrote to Francis Thompson, for
whom he had a special regard not only as a fellow-poet but
as a fellow-worshipper of Alice Meynell, to say that if he
was seriously ill he would come and look after him, adding
that it would be a great pleasure and honour to serve him
in any way.

But his own case was rapidly becoming the more serious.
He retained his habits and his interests, but his body dragged
along behind them. It was one of his habits to go and read
the papers each morning in the Angel Hotel at Lymington,
but at last he was so weak that he could only get along there
in his dressing-gown, the odd costume which Balzac, another
great independent whose basic ideas were not dissimilar to
his own, had made his working dress. Patmore's biographer
called this "a picturesque but unconventional garb."

Picturesque and unconventional he remained, even keeping to his walks in the darkness, a habit he had developed
from night walks on the shore at Hastings. At the return from
one of these walks in the November of 1896 he was more
exhausted than usual, and of the doctor, summoned next
morning, he enquired—with his usual optimism, "What
about going to Heaven this time?" Pressed, the doctor admitted that his case was serious. But when the priest paused
in saying the prayers for the dying he had the strength to
repeat a phrase.

He died at four o'clock in the afternoon of November
26th, 1896, at the age of seventy-three.

At the passage of the funeral the Anglican church bell was tolling and the clergyman stood uncovered at the door, a generous tribute to one whose religious sympathies had not only extended beyond his own communion, but beyond Christianity itself, finding an echo of its richer truth in the words, "Happy is he who understands the mystery of Persephone. Over such an one Hades has no power."

Even the obelisk which surmounts Patmore's tomb in Lymington cemetery commemorates an older mystery, the coming of the Israelites and the Messiah out of Egypt, the release of the spirit from the bondage of the flesh.

No cross marks his grave, nor was his the way of the Cross, yet it may well be true that after the great tragedy of his life, the death of Emily Patmore, he had to "crucify his heart," as he wrote in one of his odes, and submit to "bliss in which she had no part." Such submission is not always the easier choice to men who remember happiness more often than they contemplate its presence, for there are some who are condemned to life as others are condemned to death.

It was some twenty years before his death that Coventry Patmore had written hopefully of the dying hour when he could at last say, "My only, only Love, O, take me back again."

His meditations on human and divine love were the stuff of the man, and many will find a discrepancy between these exalted heights and the foothills of his life. Yet this disappointing gap shows at every level of human experience. A man who has climbed Mount Everest figures in the imagination as a hero, and those who meet him on the lower levels of a party may sometimes be disconcerted to find that he is a man. Men are not less great for being human. No artist has painted a Christ who strikes the eye as overwhelmingly different from other men, yet such paintings at least emphasize that the God was also a man. Among Christians and sinners there is another contrast between the inner vision and the flesh's reality. Though Coventry Patmore appeared to Gosse an "extraordinary man," there was also a very ordinary man in him. He had climbed the mountain of revelation, and like Moses he had also descended from it.

At least he had seen the light that comes into the world, nor had he denied in the darkness what he had seen in the light.

Note on Sources

The well from which every critic of Patmore has to draw is Basil Champneys' *Memoirs and Correspondence of Coventry Patmore* (two volumes, Bell, 1900). This was limited by the conventions of the time and the reticence of the third Mrs. Patmore, but as a friend who had enjoyed Patmore's frankness Champneys grasped some nettles, such as Patmore's anti-clericalism, more firmly than is usual with official biographers.

But even Champneys needs supplementing by Mr. Derek Patmore's *Life and Times of Coventry Patmore* (Constable, 1949), a study so complete and so recent that it would be impertinent to add more, had not the author expressly stated that it was not his aim to deal with Coventry Patmore's work. Mr. Derek Patmore's work is particularly valuable because of his access to family papers and his treatment of Alice Meynell and the third Mrs. Patmore, about whom he was able to say more than was possible in 1900.

On Patmore's work and temperament Edmund Gosse, in his *Coventry Patmore* (Hodder and Stoughton, 1905), is admirably balanced between the cordiality of a friend and the detachment of a critic.

The best treatment of Patmore's views is provided by Osbert Burdett's *The Idea of Coventry Patmore* (Oxford University Press, 1921), unique in that nearly half of the book. is devoted to *The Angel in the House.* Burdett was also the first critic to relate Patmore's poetry closely to his prose, but did not attempt to relate either to his life.

Much the best short account of Patmore is that given by Valéry Larbaud and republished in his "Ce Vice Impuni, La Lecture . . . Domaine Anglais" (*Nouvelle Revue Francaise*, 1936). M. Larbaud, besides being an outstanding writer, is also the most lucid and fervent interpreter of English literature. His essay, scholarly and rich in facts, is even richer in discernment and sympathy.

Other essays on Patmore have been written by Frank Harris, Sir Herbert Read, and Mr. Peter Quennell. Harris' essay is laudatory, not free from his tendency to turn every essay on another man into an autobiographical extract, but it has his own eccentric illumination. Sir Herbert Read's is important as the first revaluation of a great Victorian, and in its insistence on *The Rod, the Root, and the Flower* as a masterpiece. Mr. Quennell's essay is useful as that of a hostile critic unable to accept the contrast between Patmore's views and his life.

A very full bibliography of writings on Patmore (which also includes works by his father) is given at the end of Mr. Derek Patmore's *Life and Times of Coventry Patmore*, to which the student is referred.

Verse extracts in the text are from the Bell edition of the *Poems*, first published in 1906. Quotations from *Principle in Art* and *Religio Poetae* are from the Duckworth Readers' Library edition of 1913; from *The Rod, the Root, and the Flower*, from the Bell edition of 1923.

Index